The Apologia of Apuleius of Madaura

Apuleius

Alpha Editions

This edition published in 2024

ISBN : 9789367245446

Design and Setting By
Alpha Editions
www.alphaedis.com
Email - info@alphaedis.com

As per information held with us this book is in Public Domain.
This book is a reproduction of an important historical work. Alpha Editions uses the best technology to reproduce historical work in the same manner it was first published to preserve its original nature. Any marks or number seen are left intentionally to preserve its true form.

Contents

INTRODUCTION ....- 1 -
THE APOLOGIA ....- 8 -
THE FLORIDA ....- 79 -
NOTES..- 108 -
FOOTNOTES ....- 124 -

INTRODUCTION

OUR authorities for the life of Apuleius are in the main the *Apologia*, the *Florida*, and the last book of the *Metamorphoses*. He has a passion for taking his audience into his confidence, and as a result it is not hard to reconstruct a considerable portion of his life. He was a native of Madaura, the modern Mdaurusch, a Numidian town loftily situated above the valley of the Medjerda. The town was a flourishing Roman colony (*Apol.* 24), and the family of Apuleius was among the wealthiest and most important of the town. His father attained to the position of *duumvir*, the highest municipal office (*Apol.* loc. cit.), and left his son the considerable fortune of 2,000,000 sesterces (£20,000). As to the date of Apuleius' birth there is some uncertainty. But as he was the fellow student (*Florida* 16) at Rome of Aemilianus Strabo (consul 156 A.D.), and was considerably younger than his wife Pudentilla, whom he married about 155 A.D., when she had 'barely passed the age of forty' (*Apol.* 89), the estimate which places his birth about 125 A.D. cannot be far wrong. His name is generally given as Lucius Apuleius, though the only authority for the *praenomen* is the evidence of late MSS., and it is not improbable that the origin of the name is to be found in the curious identification of himself with Lucius, the hero of the *Metamorphoses* (xi. 27). At an early age the young Apuleius was sent to school at Carthage (*Florida* 18), whence on attaining to manhood he proceeded to complete his education at Athens (*Florida* loc. cit.). There he studied philosophy, rhetoric, geometry, music, and poetry (*Florida* 20), and laid the foundations of that encyclopaedic, if superficial knowledge, which in after years he so delighted to parade. On leaving Athens he set forth on lengthy travels, in the course of which he spent a large portion of his patrimony (*Apol.* 23). He speaks of the temple of Hera at Samos as an eyewitness (*Florida* 15), and elsewhere mentions a visit to Hierapolis in Phrygia (*de mundo* 17). Returning from the East he came to Corinth, where—if we may accept his identification of himself with the Lucius of the *Metamorphoses*—he fell into the clutches of the priests of Isis, who played upon his emotional and superstitious temperament to their hearts' content. He was first initiated into the mysteries of Isis (*Metamorph.* xi. 23, 24). A few days after this auspicious event the goddess appeared to him in a vision and bade him set forth homewards. He therefore took ship for Rome, where for the space of a year he dwelt, a fervent worshipper at the temple of Isis on the Campus Martius. Once more visions of the night began to afflict him; he consulted the priests and discovered the cause; he required yet to be initiated into the mysteries of Osiris. The priests of Corinth had worked upon his credulity to such good effect, that he found himself in serious financial difficulties, but by practising as a lawyer he succeeded in making a sufficient income to provide more than adequately for the expenses of this fresh initiation (*Metamorph.* xi. 28, 30). While at Rome he made the acquaintance of Aemilianus Strabo and Scipio Orfitus, men of distinguished position, whom he was to meet again when their official career brought them to Africa as proconsuls of that province (*Florida* 16, 17).

At last he returned home, and it was probably at this period of his career that he wrote his famous novel, the *Metamorphoses* or *Golden Ass*.[1] It is based on the lost work of a certain Lucius of Patras, of which we have another version in the Λούκιος ἢ ὄνος, falsely attributed to Lucian. He enlarged the original by the free insertion of sensational or humorous stories of the kind popularized later by the *Decameron* of Boccaccio, above all by the insertion of the beautiful fairy-tale of Cupid and Psyche. And then at the end comes the curious personal note, where Lucius, a Greek at the outset of the romance, becomes strangely transformed into a native of Madaura.

But he did not settle down in his native town. After a time he visited Alexandria, and it was in the course of his return from the capital of Egypt that the crisis in his life occurred, to which we owe that remarkable human document, the *Apologia*. For on his homeward journey he fell sick at Oea, the modern Tripoli.[2] In this town there dwelt a wealthy lady, named Aemilia Pudentilla, the widow of Sicinius Amicus, by whom she had two sons, Sicinius Pontianus and his younger brother, Sicinius Pudens. Pontianus was already the friend of Apuleius; he had made his acquaintance at Athens; an intimacy had sprung up between them, and they had lived together in the same lodgings. Hearing, therefore, of Apuleius' sickness, he called on him at the house of their mutual friends the Appii, where he was lodging. The reasons for Pontianus' visit were somewhat remarkable. His grandfather had been anxious that Pudentilla should take a second husband in the person of his son and her brother-in-law, Sicinius Clarus, and with this end in view threatened to exclude her sons, whose guardian he was, from the possession of any of their father's property, if she married elsewhere. She therefore suffered herself to be betrothed to Sicinius Clarus, 'a boorish and decrepit old man,' but put off the marriage, until her father-in-law's death released her from all embarrassment. Pontianus and Pudens succeeded to the property, and Pudentilla felt herself free to take a husband of her own choice. She informed her sons of her intentions. Pontianus approved, but since the property left to himself and Pudens by their grandfather was small, and all his expectations of wealth depended on the ultimate inheritance of his mother's fortune (4,000,000 sesterces = £40,000), he was most anxious that his mother should marry an honest man who might reasonably be expected to treat his step-sons fairly. At this point, in the very nick of time, Apuleius was detained at Oea. Pontianus saw in him a heaven-sent step-father, and it was with this in his mind that he called upon Apuleius. He did not declare his intentions at once. He contented himself at first with dissuading Apuleius from pursuing his journey homeward till the next winter came round, and persuaded him to come and stay in his mother's house. Apuleius accepted his offer and their old intimacy revived. At last a suitable occasion offered for the declaration of Pontianus' wishes. Apuleius had given a public lecture at Oea. His audience broke into frenzied applause and begged Apuleius to become a citizen of their town.

When the audience were gone, Pontianus took Apuleius aside and, saying that the popular enthusiasm was a sign from heaven, begged Apuleius to marry Pudentilla. After much deliberation Apuleius consented, though the lady was neither fair to view nor young. She had been a widow for more than thirteen years, and was now over forty. Soon, however, he began to love Pudentilla for her own sake; her virtues and intelligence won his heart and overcame his desire for further travel. The marriage was duly solemnized. But it brought Apuleius no peace. Sicinius Aemilianus, another brother of her first husband, and Herennius Rufinus, the disreputable father-in-law of Pontianus, were both up in arms. Rufinus had hoped, through his son-in-law, to reap a rich harvest from Pudentilla's fortune; Aemilianus resented the treatment of his brother, Sicinius Clarus. They sought, therefore, how they might have their revenge. Their first step was to win Pontianus and Pudens to their side. This they succeeded in doing, in spite of the generous treatment accorded by Apuleius to his step-sons. Pontianus fell sick and died before they could carry out their designs. He had, moreover, repented of his baseness to his former friend, though death prevented him from showing what his repentance was worth. Pudens, however, was completely under the thumb of Aemilianus and Rufinus, and a number of more or less serious charges were brought against Apuleius in his name.

He was accused of having won the heart of Pudentilla by sorcery, of being a man of immoral life, and of having married his elderly bride solely for the sake of her money. The trial took place at Sabrata (*Apol.* 59), the modern Zowâra, lying on the coast some sixty miles west of Oea. The case was tried by the proconsul himself, Claudius Maximus. The date cannot be precisely fixed. But Claudius Maximus was probably proconsul at some time between the years 155-158 A.D. (see note on *Apol.* 1), at any rate not later than 161 A.D., since Antoninus Pius is mentioned as the reigning princeps (died March 161 A.D.). Apuleius had no difficulty in disposing of the charges brought against him, and incidentally found an opportunity for a flamboyant display of the learning of which he was so proud. He may well on occasion have practised magic: his insatiable curiosity must assuredly have led him to experiment in this direction, and his subsequent reputation confirms these suspicions. But the specific charges of magic on this occasion were frivolous and absurd. In the first portion of the speech Apuleius plays with his accusers, mocking them from the heights of his superior learning. In the second portion, where he defends his marriage with Pudentilla and justifies his dealings with his step-sons, he clears himself in good earnest, nay does more than clear himself. For he unveils in the most merciless fashion the villany of his accusers—the base ingratitude of Pudens, and the unspeakable turpitude of Rufinus.

That Apuleius was acquitted cannot be doubted. His case speaks for itself. But it is noteworthy that we hear of him no more at Oea, where he had resided for three years at the time of the trial. This distressing family quarrel must have caused some bitterness of feeling, and Augustine (*Ep.* 138. 19) mentions a quarrel with the inhabitants of Oea on the question of the erection of a statue in his honour. These facts may not improbably have led him to seek residence elsewhere. Be this as it may, when we next hear of him he is in Carthage, enjoying the highest renown as philosopher, poet, and rhetorician. It was during this residence at Carthage that he delivered the flamboyant orations of which fragments have been preserved to us in the *Florida*. A few of these excerpts can be dated. The seventeenth is written during the proconsulate of Scipio Orfitus in 163-164 A.D. The ninth contains a panegyric of the proconsul Severianus, who must have held office some time during the joint reign of Marcus Aurelius and Lucius Verus, 161-169 A.D. (see note, p. 236). The sixteenth refers to Aemilianus Strabo, who was consul in 156 A.D. and had not yet become proconsul of Africa. As the interval between holding the consulate and the proconsulate was from ten to thirteen years, this fragment may be dated, if not before 166, at any rate before 169 A.D.

Apuleius won more than mere applause. Carthage decreed a statue in his honour (*Florida* 16), and conferred on him the chief-priesthood of the province. This office entitled its holder to the first place in the provincial council, and was the highest honour that the province could bestow (*Florida* 16). Civil office he never held (Augustine, *Ep.* 138. 19), perhaps never sought. His genius, it may be said with confidence, was far from fitting him for judicial or administrative functions. If we may trust Apollinaris Sidonius (*Ep.* II. 10. 5), Pudentilla showed herself a model wife by the passionate interest she took in her husband's work. 'Pudentilla was for Apuleius what Marcia was for Hortensius, Terentia for Cicero, Calpurnia for Piso, Rusticiana for Symmachus: these noble women held the lamp while their husbands read and meditated!' It is even possible that she bore him a son, as the second book of the *de Platone* is dedicated to 'my son Faustinus'. Of his death we know nothing. Testimony as to his appearance is conflicting. His accusers (*Apol.* 4) charge him with being a 'handsome philosopher'. He replies that his body is worn by the fatigues of study and his hair as tangled as a lump of tow!

His works were astonishingly numerous. Beside those already mentioned there have come down to us two books on the life and philosophy of Plato,[3] a highly rhetorical treatise on the 'Demon of Socrates', and a free translation of the pseudo-Aristotelian treatise 'on the Universe', though Apuleius is regrettably far from making due acknowledgement of his debt to the original. None of these works can be described as interesting, though the treatise on the 'Demon of Socrates' contains some characteristic purple passages.

It would, however, scarcely be an exaggeration to say that more of Apuleius' works have perished than survived. He has told us in the *Florida* (20) that he has written dialogues, hymns, music, history, and satire. And we have copious references to works from his pen, that, perhaps fortunately, no longer exist. Beside the three poems which survive in the *Apologia* and a translation of a passage of Menander, preserved in a manuscript once at Beauvais, but now lost (Baehrens, *Poet. Lat. Min.* 4, p. 104), he mentions a hymn to Aesculapius, written both in Latin and Greek (*Florida* 18), and a panegyric in verse on the virtues of Scipio Orfitus (*Florida* 17). He wrote also another novel entitled *Hermagoras*, a collection of famous love-stories of the past, sundry 'histories', a translation of the *Phaedo*, and numerous scientific works, dealing with problems of mathematics, music, astronomy, medicine, botany, and zoology.

The glory won by Apuleius during his lifetime survived after his death. Augustine knows his works well. He recognizes his importance as a writer, but abhors him as a magician. Apuleius is a thaumaturge against whom the faithful need to be warned. 'The enemies of Christianity,' says Augustine (*Ep.* 138), 'venture to place Apuleius and Apollonius of Tyana on the same or even a higher level than Christ.' But in the same letter he speaks of him as a 'great orator' whose fame still lives among his fellow countrymen of Africa. Above all the *Golden Ass* has kept his name alive to our own day. Even those who know nothing of the work as a whole, or who would relegate it to obscurity for its occasional gross indecency, know and love the story of Cupid and Psyche, if not in the original at least in many a work of art, and in the pages of La Fontaine, Walter Pater, or William Morris.

As might be expected from one who left so few themes untouched, Apuleius is one of the most superficial of ancient writers. It has been well said of him by M. Paul Monceaux, 'Apulée est un de ces esprits encyclopédiques, âpres à la curée de toutes les connaissances, qui se rencontrent au commencement et à la fin des civilisations.' For the acquisition of his extraordinary reputation he needed an age and an audience in which learning and literature alike were decadent, though far from forgotten. He has none of the scientific spirit. He does not really understand the authors he quotes; he has no critical spirit, and his own investigations are prompted by indiscriminate curiosity. But he has vast stores of miscellaneous knowledge such as might delight the half-educated, and as a rhetorician he possesses a strange and debased brilliance, fired by an astonishing if disorderly imagination. The verve, the humour, and above all the welter of warmth and colour that characterize the *Golden Ass* make us forgive the palpable degradation of the Latin language. Not less remarkable is the *Apologia*. There are few speeches of antiquity that give such a vivid impression of the character of the author and of the life of the society in which he moved. The style, it is true, is often bombastic and affected, many of the arguments are almost more puerile and absurd than the accusations, while the intense conceit and complacency of the author often make him ridiculous. A man of wide and varied knowledge, he has no depth of intellect. He is always half charlatan, and the reader is rarely free from the impression that he is taking liberties with the uncertain taste and ignorance of his provincial audience. But even the weaknesses of style and argument have their charm for the modern reader. For, if he never entirely fails to laugh with Apuleius, he certainly indulges in many a hearty laugh at him.

The *Florida* are no less superficial and bombastic, and the vanity of Apuleius is revealed even more remarkably than in the *Apologia*. But they are never long enough to be tedious, and contain much that is amusing, be the humour unconscious or intentional; and even if we can rarely give whole-hearted admiration to the style, we cannot but marvel at its dexterity, while its very *bizarrerie* is not without its charm.

This is hardly the place for a disquisition upon African Latin. It is sufficient here to say that the two main features of the style of Apuleius are its archaism and its extreme floridity. It has been asserted that this strange style is of purely African growth,[4] and that it owes much of its oriental wealth of colour to the Semitic element that must still have formed so large a proportion of the population of Africa. But there seems little really to support this view; it is probable that, allowing for the personal factor, in this case exceptionally important, and the eccentricities to which Apuleius' erudition may have led him, we are confronted with no more than an exaggerated revival of the Asiatic style of oratory. No doubt the seed fell on good ground, but it is impossible to set one's finger on any definitely African element.[5]

The style presents grave difficulties to the translator. The English language will not carry the requisite amount of bombast; the assonances and the puns are generally incapable of reproduction. Even when this allowance has been made, it is in many cases impossible to give anything approximating to a translation in natural English. I can only trust that the English of this translation has not wholly lost the colour to which Apuleius owes so much of his charm. The sacrifice is not so great in these works as it must necessarily be in any English translation of the more exotic and more brilliant-hued

Metamorphoses, better known as *The Golden Ass*. But in any case the cooler tints and sobriety of our native language must—even in hands less unskilled than mine—fail to do justice to the fantastic Latin of the original. The vivacity of French coupled with the richness and warmth of Italian would need to be combined to produce anything approaching a really good translation, even of the least fantastic works of Apuleius.

THE APOLOGIA

1. FOR my part, Maximus Claudius, and you, gentlemen who sit beside him on the bench, I regarded it as a foregone conclusion that Sicinius Aemilianus would for sheer lack of any real ground for accusation cram his indictment with mere vulgar abuse; for the old rascal is notorious for his unscrupulous audacity, and, further, launched forth on his task of bringing me to trial in your court before he had given a thought to the line his prosecution should pursue. Now while the most innocent of men may be the victim of false accusation, only the criminal can have his guilt brought home to him. It is this thought that gives me special confidence, but I have further ground for self-congratulation in the fact that I have you for my judge on an occasion when it is my privilege to have the opportunity of clearing philosophy of the aspersions cast upon her by the uninstructed and of proving my own innocence. Nevertheless these false charges are on the face of them serious enough, and the suddenness with which they have been improvised makes them the more difficult to refute. For you will remember that it is only four or five days since his advocates of malice prepense attacked me with slanderous accusations, and began to charge me with practice of the black art and with the murder of my step-son Pontianus. I was at the moment totally unprepared for such a charge, and was occupied in defending an action brought by the brothers Granius against my wife, Pudentilla. I perceived that these charges were brought forward not so much in a serious spirit as to gratify my opponents' taste for wanton slander. I therefore straightway challenged them, not once only, but frequently and emphatically, to proceed with their accusation. The result was that Aemilianus, perceiving that you, Maximus, not to speak of others, were strongly moved by what had occurred, and that his words had created a serious scandal, began to be alarmed and to seek for some safe refuge from the consequences of his rashness.

2. Therefore as soon as he was compelled to set his name to the indictment, he conveniently forgot Pontianus, his own brother's son, of whose death he had been continually accusing me only a few days previously. He made absolutely no mention of the death of his young kinsman[6]; he abandoned this most serious charge, but—to avoid the appearance of having totally abandoned his mendacious accusations—he selected, as the sole support of his indictment, the charge of magic—a charge with which it is easy to create a prejudice against the accused, but which it is hard to prove. Even that he had not the courage to do openly in his own person, but a day later presented the indictment in the name of my step-son, Sicinius Pudens, a mere boy, adding that he appeared as his representative. This is a new method. He attacks me through the agency of a third person, whose tender age he

employs to shield his unworthy self against a charge of false accusation. You, Maximus, with great acuteness saw through his designs and ordered him to renew his original accusation in person. In spite of his promise to comply, he cannot be induced to come to close quarters, but actually defies your authority and continues to skirmish at long range with his false accusations. He persistently shirks the perilous task of a direct attack, and perseveres in his assumption of the safe rôle of the accuser's legal representative. As a result, even before the case came into court, the real nature of the accusation became obvious to the meanest understanding. The man who invented the charge and was the first to utter it had not the courage to take the responsibility for it. Moreover the man in question is Sicinius Aemilianus, who, if he had discovered any true charge against me, would scarcely have been so backward in accusing a stranger of so many serious crimes, seeing that he falsely asserted his own uncle's will to be a forgery although he knew it to be genuine: indeed he maintained this assertion with such obstinate violence, that even after that distinguished senator, Lollius Urbicus, in accordance with the decision of the distinguished consulars, his assessors, had declared the will to be genuine and duly proven, he continued—such was his mad fury—in defiance of the award given by the voice of that most distinguished citizen, to assert with oaths that the will was a forgery. It was only with difficulty that Lollius Urbicus refrained from making him suffer for it.

3. I rely, Maximus, on your sense of justice and on my own innocence, but I hope that in this trial also we shall hear the voice of Lollius raised impulsively in my defence; for Aemilianus is deliberately accusing a man whom he knows to be innocent, a course which comes the more easy to him, since, as I have told you, he has already been convicted of lying in a most important case, heard before the Prefect of the city. Just as a good man studiously avoids the repetition of a sin once committed, so men of depraved character repeat their past offence with increased confidence, and, I may add, the more often they do so, the more openly they display their impudence. For honour is like a garment; the older it gets, the more carelessly it is worn. I think it my duty, therefore, in the interest of my own honour, to refute all my opponent's slanders before I come to the actual indictment itself. For I am pleading not merely my own cause, but that of philosophy as well, philosophy, whose grandeur is such that she resents even the slightest slur cast upon her perfection as though it were the most serious accusation. Knowing this, Aemilianus' advocates, only a short time ago, poured forth with all their usual loquacity a flood of drivelling accusations, many of which were specially invented for the purpose of blackening my character, while the remainder were such general charges as the uninstructed are in the habit of levelling at philosophers. It is true that we may regard these accusations as mere interested vapourings, bought at a price and uttered to prove their

shamelessness worthy of its hire. It is a recognized practice on the part of professional accusers to let out the venom of their tongues to another's hurt; nevertheless, if only in my own interest, I must briefly refute these slanders, lest I, whose most earnest endeavour it is to avoid incurring the slightest spot or blemish to my fair fame, should seem, by passing over some of their more ridiculous charges, to have tacitly admitted their truth, rather than to have treated them with silent contempt. For a man who has any sense of honour or self-respect must needs—such at least is my opinion—feel annoyed when he is thus abused, however falsely. Even those whose conscience reproaches them with some crime, are strongly moved to anger, when men speak ill of them, although they have been accustomed to such ill report ever since they became evildoers. And even though others say naught of their crimes, they are conscious enough that such charges may at any time deservedly be brought against them. It is therefore doubly vexatious to the good and innocent man when charges are undeservedly brought against him which he might with justice bring against others. For his ears are unused and strange to ill report, and he is so accustomed to hear himself praised that insult is more than he can bear. If, however, I seem to be anxious to rebut charges which are merely frivolous and foolish, the blame must be laid at the door of those, to whom such accusations, in spite of their triviality, can only bring disgrace. I am not to blame. Ridiculous as these charges may be, their refutation cannot but do me honour.

4. To begin then, only a short while ago, at the commencement of the indictment, you heard them say, 'He, whom we accuse in your court, is a philosopher of the most elegant appearance and a master of eloquence not merely in Latin but also in Greek!' What a damning insinuation! Unless I am mistaken, those were the very words with which Tannonius Pudens, whom no one could accuse of being a master of eloquence, began the indictment. I wish that these serious reproaches of beauty and eloquence had been true. It would have been easy to answer in the words, with which Homer makes Paris reply to Hector:—

οὔ τοι ἀπόβλητ' ἐστὶ θεῶν ἐρικυδέα δῶρα·
ὅσσα κεν αὐτοὶ δῶσιν, ἑκὼν δ' οὐκ ἄν τις ἕλοιτο.—

which I may interpret thus: 'The most glorious gifts of the gods are in no wise to be despised; but the things which they are wont to give are withheld from many that would gladly possess them.' Such would have been my reply. I should have added that philosophers are not forbidden to possess a handsome face. Pythagoras, the first to take the name of 'philosopher', was the handsomest man of his day. Zeno also, the ancient philosopher of Velia, who was the first to discover that most ingenious device of refuting hypotheses by the method of self-inconsistency, that same Zeno was—so

Plato asserts—by far the most striking in appearance of all the men of his generation. It is further recorded of many other philosophers that they were comely of countenance and added fresh charm to their personal beauty by their beauty of character. But such a defence is, as I have already said, far from me. Not only has nature given me but a commonplace appearance, but continued literary labour has swept away such charm as my person ever possessed, has reduced me to a lean habit of body, sucked away all the freshness of life, destroyed my complexion and impaired my vigour. As to my hair, which they with unblushing mendacity declare I have allowed to grow long as an enhancement to my personal attractions, you can judge of its elegance and beauty. As you see, it is tangled, twisted and unkempt like a lump of tow, shaggy and irregular in length, so knotted and matted that the tangle is past the art of man to unravel. This is due not to mere carelessness in the tiring of my hair, but to the fact that I never so much as comb or part it. I think this is a sufficient refutation of the accusations concerning my hair which they hurl against me as though it were a capital charge.

5. As to my eloquence—if only eloquence were mine—it would be small matter either for wonder or envy if I, who from my earliest years to the present moment have devoted myself with all my powers to the sole study of literature and for this spurned all other pleasures, had sought to win eloquence to be mine with toil such as few or none have ever expended, ceasing neither night nor day, to the neglect and impairment of my bodily health. But my opponents need fear nothing from my eloquence. If I have made any real advance therein, it is my aspirations rather than my attainments on which I must base my claim. Certainly if the aphorism said to occur in the poems of Statius Caecilius be true, that innocence is eloquence itself, to that extent I may lay claim to eloquence and boast that I yield to none. For on that assumption what living man could be more eloquent than myself? I have never even harboured in my thoughts anything to which I should fear to give utterance. Nay, my eloquence is consummate, for I have ever held all sin in abomination; I have the highest oratory at my command, for I have uttered no word, I have done no deed, of which I need fear to discourse in public. I will begin therefore to discourse of those verses of mine, which they have produced as though they were something of which I ought to be ashamed. You must have noticed the laughter with which I showed my annoyance at the absurd and illiterate manner in which they recited them.

6. They began by reading one of my *jeux d'esprit*, a brief letter in verse, addressed to a certain Calpurnianus on the subject of a tooth-powder. When Calpurnianus produced my letter as evidence against me, his desire to do me a hurt blinded him to the fact that if anything in the letter could be urged as a reproach against me, he shared in that reproach. For the verses testify to the fact that he had asked me to send him the wherewithal to clean his teeth:

Good morrow! friend Calpurnianus, take
The salutation these swift verses make.
Wherewith I send, responsive to thy call,
A powder rare to cleanse thy teeth withal.
This delicate dust of Arab spices fine
With ivory sheen shall make thy mouth to shine,
Shall smooth the swollen gums and sweep away
The relics of the feast of yesterday.
So shall no foulness, no dark smirch be seen,
If laughter show thy teeth their lips between.

I ask you, what is there in these verses that is disgusting in point either of matter or of manner? What is there that a philosopher should be ashamed to own? Unless indeed I am to blame for sending a powder made of Arabian spices to Calpurnianus, for whom it would be more suitable that he should

Polish his teeth and ruddy gums,

as Catullus says, after the filthy fashion in vogue among the Iberians.

7. I saw a short while back that some of you could scarcely restrain your laughter, when our orator treated these views of mine on the cleansing of the teeth as a matter for savage denunciation, and condemned my administration of a tooth-powder with fiercer indignation than has ever been shown in condemning the administration of a poison. Of course it is a serious charge, and one that no philosopher can afford to despise, to say of a man that he will not allow a speck of dirt to be seen upon his person, that he will not allow any visible portion of his body to be offensive or unclean, least of all the mouth, the organ used most frequently, openly and conspicuously by man, whether to kiss a friend, to conduct a conversation, to speak in public, or to offer up prayer in some temple. Indeed speech is the prelude to every kind of action and, as the greatest of poets says, proceeds from 'the barrier of our teeth'. If there were any one present here to-day with like command of the grand style, he might say after his fashion that those above all men who have any care for their manner of speaking, should pay closer attention to their mouth than to any other portion of their body, for it is the soul's antechamber, the portal of speech, and the gathering place where thoughts assemble. I myself should say that in my poor judgement there is nothing less seemly for a free-born man with the education of a gentleman than an unwashen mouth. For man's mouth is in position exalted, to the eye conspicuous, in use eloquent. True, in wild beasts and cattle the mouth is placed low and looks downward to the feet, is in close proximity to their food and to the path they tread, and is hardly ever conspicuous save when its owner is dead or infuriated with a desire to bite. But there is no part of

man that sooner catches the eye when he is silent, or more often when he speaks.

8. I should be obliged, therefore, if my critic Aemilianus would answer me and tell me whether he is ever in the habit of washing his feet, or, if he admits that he is in the habit of so doing, whether he is prepared to argue that a man should pay more attention to the cleanliness of his feet than to that of his teeth. Certainly, if like you, Aemilianus, he never opens his mouth save to utter slander and abuse, I should advise him to pay no attention to the state of his mouth nor to attempt to remove the stains from his teeth with oriental powders: he would be better employed in rubbing them with charcoal from some funeral pyre. Least of all should he wash them with common water; rather let his guilty tongue, the chosen servant of lies and bitter words, rot in the filth and ordure that it loves! Is it reasonable, wretch, that your tongue should be fresh and clean, when your voice is foul and loathsome, or that, like the viper, you should employ snow-white teeth for the emission of dark, deadly poison? On the other hand it is only right that, just as we wash a vessel that is to hold good liquor, he who knows that his words will be at once useful and agreeable should cleanse his mouth as a prelude to speech. But why should I speak further of man? Even the crocodile, the monster of the Nile—so they tell me—opens his jaws in all innocence, that his teeth may be cleaned. For his mouth being large, tongueless, and continually open in the water, multitudes of leeches become entangled in his teeth: these, when the crocodile emerges from the river and opens his mouth, are removed by a friendly waterbird, which is allowed to insert its beak without any risk to itself.

9. But enough of this! I now come to certain other of my verses, which according to them are amatory; but so vilely and coarsely did they read them as to leave no impression save one of disgust. Now what has it to do with the malpractices of the black art, if I write poems in praise of the boys of my friend Scribonius Laetus? Does the mere fact of my being a poet make me a wizard? Who ever heard any orator produce such likely ground for suspicion, such apt conjectures, such close-reasoned argument? 'Apuleius has written verses!' If they are bad, that is something against him *qua* poet, but not *qua* philosopher. If they be good, why do you accuse him? 'But they were frivolous verses of an erotic character.' So that is the charge you bring against me? and it was a mere slip of the tongue when you indicted me for practising the black art? And yet many others have written such verse, although you may be ignorant of the fact. Among the Greeks, for instance, there was a certain Teian, there was a Lacedaemonian, a Cean, and countless others; there was even a woman, a Lesbian, who wrote with such grace and such passion that the sweetness of her song makes us forgive the impropriety of her words; among our own poets there were Aedituus, Porcius, and Catulus,

with countless others. 'But they were not philosophers.' Will you then deny that Solon was a serious man and a philosopher? Yet he is the author of that most wanton verse:

> *Longing for thy body and the kiss of thy sweet lips.*

What is there so lascivious in all my verses compared with that one line? I will say nothing of the writings of Diogenes the Cynic, of Zeno the founder of Stoicism, and many other similar instances. Let me recite my own verses afresh, that my opponents may realize that I am not ashamed of them:

> *Critias my treasure is and you,*
> *Light of my life, Charinus, too*
> *Hold in my love-tormented heart*
> *Your own inalienable part.*
> *Ah! doubt not! with redoubled spite*
> *Though fire on fire consume me quite,*
> *The flames ye kindle, boys divine,*
> *I can endure, so ye be mine.*
> *Only to each may I be dear*
> *As your own selves are, and as near;*
> *Grant only this and you shall be*
> *Dear as mine own two eyes to me.*

Now let me read you the others also which they read last as being the most intemperate in expression.

> *I lay these garlands, Critias sweet,*
> *And this my song before thy feet;*
> *Song to thyself I dedicate,*
> *Wreaths to the Angel of thy fate.*
> *The song I send to hymn the praise*
> *Of this, the best of all glad days,*
> *Whereon the circling seasons bring*
> *The glory of thy fourteenth spring;*
> *The garlands, that thy brows may shine*
> *With splendour worthy spring's and thine,*
> *That thou in boyhood's golden hours*
> *Mayst deck the flower of life with flowers.*
> *Wherefore for these bright blooms of spring*
> *Thy springtide sweet surrendering,*
> *The tribute of my love repay*
> *And all my gifts with thine outweigh.*
> *Surpass the twinèd garland's grace*
> *With arms entwined in soft embrace;*

The crimson of the rose eclipse
With kisses from thy rosy lips.
Or if thou wilt, be this my meed
And breathe thy soul into the reed;
Then shall my songs be shamed and mute
Before the music of thy flute.

10. These are the verses, Maximus, which they throw in my teeth, as though they were the work of an infamous rake and had lover's garlands and serenades for their theme. You must have noticed also that in this connexion they further attack me for calling these boys Charinus and Critias, which are not their true names. On this principle they may as well accuse Caius Catullus for calling Clodia Lesbia, Ticidas for substituting the name Perilla for that of Metella, Propertius for concealing the name Hostia beneath the pseudonym of Cynthia, and Tibullus for singing of Delia in his verse, when it was Plania who ruled his heart. For my part I should rather blame Caius Lucilius, even allowing him all the license of a satiric poet, for prostituting to the public gaze the boys Gentius and Macedo, whose real names he mentions in his verse without any attempt at concealment. How much more reserved is Mantua's poet, who, when like myself he praised the slave-boy of his friend Pollio in one of his light pastoral poems, shrinks from mentioning real names and calls himself Corydon and the boy Alexis. But Aemilianus, whose rusticity far surpasses that of the shepherds and cowherds of Vergil, who is, in fact, and always has been a boor and a barbarian, though he thinks himself far more austere than Serranus, Curius, or Fabricius, those heroes of the days of old, denies that such verses are worthy of a philosopher who is a follower of Plato. Will you persist in this attitude, Aemilianus, if I can show that my verses were modelled upon Plato? For the only verses of Plato now extant are love-elegies, the reason, I imagine, being that he burned all his other poems because they were inferior in charm and finish. Listen then to the verses written by Plato in honour of the boy Aster, though I doubt if at your age it is possible for you to learn to appreciate literature:

Thou wert the morning star among the living
Ere thy fair light had fled;—
Now having died, thou art as Hesperus giving
New light unto the dead.[7]

There is another poem by Plato dealing conjointly with the boys Alexis and Phaedrus:

I did but breathe the words 'Alexis fair',
And all men gazed on him with wondering eyes,

My soul, why point to questing beasts their prize?
'Twas thus we lost our Phaedrus; ah! beware!

Without citing any further examples I will conclude by quoting a line addressed by Plato to Dion of Syracuse:

Dion, with love thou hast distraught my soul.

11. Which of us is most to blame? I who am fool enough to speak seriously of such things in a law-court? or you who are slanderous enough to include such charges in your indictment? For sportive effusions in verse are valueless as evidence of a poet's morals. Have you not read Catullus, who replies thus to those who wish him ill:

A virtuous poet must be chaste. Agreed.
But for his verses there is no such need.

The divine Hadrian, when he honoured the tomb of his friend the poet Voconius with an inscription in verse from his own pen, wrote thus:

Thy verse was wanton, but thy soul was chaste,

words which he would never have written had he regarded verse of somewhat too lively a wit as proving their author to be a man of immoral life. I remember that I have read not a few poems by the divine Hadrian himself which were of the same type. Come now, Aemilianus, I dare you to say that that was ill done which was done by an emperor and censor, the divine Hadrian, and once done was recorded for subsequent generations. But, apart from that, do you imagine that Maximus will censure anything that has Plato for its model, Plato whose verses, which I have just read, are all the purer for being frank, all the more modest for being outspoken? For in these matters and the like, dissimulation and concealment is the mark of the sinner, open acknowledgement and publication a sign that the writer is but exercising his wit. For nature has bestowed on innocence a voice wherewith to speak, but to guilt she has given silence to veil its sin.

12. I say nothing of those lofty and divine Platonic doctrines, that are familiar to but few of the elect and wholly unknown to all the uninitiate, such for instance as that which teaches us that Venus is not one goddess, but two, each being strong in her own type of love and several types of lovers. The one is the goddess of the common herd, who is fired by base and vulgar passion and commands not only the hearts of men, but cattle and wild beasts also, to give themselves over to the gratification of their desires: she strikes down these creatures with fierce intolerable force and fetters their servile bodies in the embraces of lust. The other is a celestial power endued with lofty and generous passion: she cares for none save men, and of them but

few; she neither stings nor lures her followers to foul deeds. Her love is neither wanton nor voluptuous, but serious and unadorned, and wins her lovers to the pursuit of virtue by revealing to them how fair a thing is nobility of soul. Or, if ever she commends beautiful persons to their admiration, she puts a bar upon all indecorous conduct. For the only claim that physical beauty has upon the admiration is that it reminds those whose souls have soared above things human to things divine, of that beauty which once they beheld in all its truth and purity enthroned among the gods in heaven. Wherefore let us admit that Afranius shows his usual beauty of expression when he says:

Only the sage can love, only desire
Is known to others;

although if you would know the real truth, Aemilianus, or if you are capable of ever comprehending such high matters, the sage does not love, but only remembers.

13. I would therefore beg you to pardon the philosopher Plato for his amatory verse, and relieve me of the necessity of offending against the precepts put by Ennius into the mouth of Neoptolemus by philosophizing at undue length; on the other hand if you refuse to pardon Plato, I am quite ready to suffer blame on this count in his company. I must express my deep gratitude to you, Maximus, for listening with such close attention to these side issues, which are necessary to my defence inasmuch as I am paying back my accusers in their own coin. Your kindness emboldens me to make this further request, that you will listen to all that I have to say by way of prelude to my answer to the main charge with the same courtesy and attention that you have hitherto shown.

I beg this, since I have next to deal with that long oration, austere as any censor's, which Pudens delivered on the subject of my mirror. He nearly exploded, so violently did he declaim against the horrid nature of my offence. 'The philosopher owns a mirror, the philosopher actually possesses a mirror.' Grant that I possess it: if I denied it, you might really think that your accusation had gone home: still it is by no means a necessary inference that I am in the habit of adorning myself before a mirror. Why! suppose I possessed a theatrical wardrobe, would you venture to argue from that that I am in the frequent habit of wearing the trailing robes of tragedy, the saffron cloak of the mimic dance, or the patchwork suit of the harlequinade? I think not. On the contrary there are plenty of things of which I enjoy the use without the possession. But if possession is no proof of use nor non-possession of non-use, and if you complain of the fact that I look into the mirror rather than that I possess it, you must go on to show when and in whose presence I have ever looked into it; for as things stand, you make it a greater crime for a philosopher to look upon a mirror than for the uninitiated to gaze upon the mystic emblems of Ceres.

14. Come now, let me admit that I *have* looked into it. Is it a crime to be acquainted with one's own likeness and to carry it with one wherever one goes ready to hand within the compass of a small mirror, instead of keeping it hidden away in some one place? Are you ignorant of the fact that there is nothing more pleasing for a man to look upon than his own image? At any rate I know that fathers love those sons most who most resemble themselves, and that public statues are decreed as a reward for merit that the original may gladden his heart by looking on them. What else is the significance of statues and portraits produced by the various arts? You will scarcely maintain the paradox that what is worthy of admiration when produced by art is blameworthy when produced by nature; for nature has an even greater facility and truth than art. Long labour is expended over all the portraits wrought by the hand of man, yet they never attain to such truth as is revealed by a mirror. Clay is lacking in life, marble in colour, painting in solidity, and all three in motion, which is the most convincing element in a likeness: whereas in a mirror the reflection of the image is marvellous, for it is not only like its original, but moves and follows every nod of the man to whom it belongs; its age always corresponds to that of those who look into the mirror, from their earliest childhood to their expiring age: it puts on all the changes brought by the advance of years, shares all the varying habits of the body, and imitates the shifting expressions of joy and sorrow that may be seen on the face of one and the same man. For all we mould in clay or cast in bronze or carve in stone or tint with encaustic pigments or colour with paint, in a word, every attempt at artistic representation by the hand of man after a brief lapse of time loses its truth and becomes motionless and impassive like the face of a corpse. So far superior to all pictorial art in respect of truthful representation is the craftsmanship of the smooth mirror and the splendour of its art.

15. Two alternatives then are before us. We must either follow the precept of the Lacedaemonian Agesilaus, who had no confidence in his personal appearance and refused to allow his portrait to be painted or carved; or we must accept the universal custom of the rest of mankind which welcomes portraiture both in sculpture and painting. In the latter case, is there any reason for preferring to see one's portrait moulded in marble rather than reflected in silver, in a painting rather than in a mirror? Or do you regard it as disgraceful to pay continual attention to one's own appearance? Is not Socrates said actually to have urged his followers frequently to consider their image in a glass, that so those of them that prided themselves on their appearance might above all else take care that they did no dishonour to the splendour of their body by the blackness of their hearts; while those who

regarded themselves as less than handsome in personal appearance might take especial pains to conceal the meanness of their body by the glory of their virtue? You see; the wisest man of his day actually went so far as to use the mirror as an instrument of moral discipline. Again, who is ignorant of the fact that Demosthenes, the greatest master of the art of speaking, always practised pleading before a mirror as though before a professor of rhetoric? When that supreme orator had drained deep draughts of eloquence in the study of Plato the philosopher, and had learned all that could be learned of argumentation from the dialectician Eubulides, last of all he betook himself to a mirror to learn perfection of delivery. Which do you think should pay greatest attention to the decorousness of his appearance in the delivery of a speech? The orator when he wrangles with his opponent or the philosopher when he rebukes the vices of mankind? The man who harangues for a brief space before an audience of jurymen drawn by the chance of the lot, or he who is continually discoursing with all mankind for audience? The man who is quarrelling over the boundaries of lands, or he whose theme is the boundaries of good and evil? Moreover there are other reasons why a philosopher should look into a mirror. He is not always concerned with the contemplation of his own likeness, he contemplates also the causes which produce that likeness. Is Epicurus right when he asserts that images proceed forth from us, as it were a kind of slough that continually streams from our bodies? These images when they strike anything smooth and solid are reflected by the shock and reversed in such wise as to give back an image turned to face its original. Or should we accept the view maintained by other philosophers that rays are emitted from our body? According to Plato these rays are filtered forth from the centre of our eyes and mingle and blend with the light of the world without us; according to Archytas they issue forth from us without any external support; according to the Stoics these rays are called into action[8] by the tension of the air: all agree that, when these emanations strike any dense, smooth, and shining surface, they return to the surface from which they proceeded in such manner that the angle of incidence is equal to the angle of reflection, and as a result that which they approach and touch without the mirror is imaged within the mirror.

16. What think you? Should not philosophers make all these problems subjects of research and inquiry and in solitary study look into mirrors of every kind, solid and liquid? There is also over and above these questions further matter for discussion. For instance, why is it that in flat mirrors all images and objects reflected are shown in almost precisely their original dimensions, whereas in convex and spherical mirrors everything is seen smaller, in concave mirrors on the other hand larger than nature? Why again and under what circumstances are left and right reversed? When does one and the same mirror seem now to withdraw the image into its depths, now to extrude it forth to view? Why do concave mirrors when held at right angles

to the rays of the sun kindle tinder set opposite them? What is the cause of the prismatic colours of the rainbow, or of the appearance in heaven of <u>two rival images of the sun</u>, with sundry other phenomena treated in a monumental volume by Archimedes of Syracuse, a man who showed extraordinary and unique subtlety in all branches of geometry, but was perhaps particularly remarkable for his frequent and attentive inspection of mirrors. If you had only read this book, Aemilianus, and, instead of devoting yourself to the study of your fields and their dull clods, had studied the mathematician's slate and blackboard, believe me, although your face is hideous enough for a tragic mask of Thyestes, you would assuredly, in your desire for the acquisition of knowledge, look into the glass and sometimes leave your plough to marvel at the numberless furrows with which wrinkles have scored your face.

But I should not be surprised if you prefer me to speak of your ugly deformity of a face and to be silent about your morals, which are infinitely more repulsive than your features. I will say nothing of them. In the first place I am not naturally of a quarrelsome disposition, and secondly I am glad to say that until quite recently you might have been white or black for all I knew. Even now my knowledge of you is inadequate. The reason for this is that your rustic occupations have kept you in obscurity, while *I* have been occupied by my studies, and so the shadow cast about you by your insignificance has shielded your character from scrutiny, while I for my part take no interest in others' ill deeds, but have always thought it more important to conceal my own faults than to track out those of others. As a result you have the advantage of one who, while he is himself shrouded in darkness, surveys another who chances to have taken his stand in the full light of day. You from your darkness can with ease form an opinion as to what I am doing in my not undistinguished position before all the world; but your position is so abject, so obscure, and so withdrawn from the light of publicity that you are by no means so conspicuous.

17. I neither know nor care to know whether you have slaves to till your fields or whether you do so by interchange of service with your neighbours. But *you* know that at Oea I gave three slaves their freedom on the same day, and your advocate has cast it in my teeth together with other actions of mine of which you have given him information. And yet but a few minutes earlier he had declared that I came to Oea accompanied by no more than one slave. I challenge you to tell me how I could have made one slave into three free men. But perhaps this is one of my feats of magic. Has lying made you blind, or shall I rather say that from force of habit you are incapable of speaking the truth? 'Apuleius,' you say, 'came to Oea with one slave,' and then only a very few words later you blurt out, 'Apuleius on one and the same day at Oea gave three slaves their freedom.' Not even the assertion that I had come with

three slaves and had given them all their freedom would have been credible: but suppose I had done so, what reason have you for regarding three slaves as a mark of my poverty, rather than for considering three freed men as a proof of my wealth? Poor Aemilianus, you have not the least idea how to accuse a philosopher: you reproach me for the scantiness of my household, whereas it would really have been my duty to have laid claim, however falsely, to such poverty. It would have redounded to my credit, for I know that not only philosophers of whom I boast myself a follower, but also generals of the Roman people have gloried in the small number of their slaves. Have your advocates really never read that [Marcus Antonius](), a man who had filled the office of consul, had but eight slaves in his house? That that very [Carbo]() who obtained supreme control of Rome had fewer by one? That [Manius Curius](), famous beyond all men for the crowns of victory that he had won, Manius Curius who thrice led the triumphal procession through the same gate of Rome, had but two servants to attend him in camp, so that in good truth that same man who triumphed over the Sabines, the Samnites, and Pyrrhus had fewer slaves than triumphs? [Marcus Cato]() did not wait for others to tell it of him, but himself records the fact in one of his speeches that when he set out as consul for Spain he took but three slaves from the city with him. When, however, he came to stay at a state residence, the number seemed insufficient, and he ordered two slaves to be bought in the market to wait on him at table, so that he took five in all to Spain. Had Pudens come across these facts in his reading, he would, I think, either have omitted this particular slander or would have preferred to reproach me on the ground that three slaves were too large rather than too small an establishment for a philosopher.

18. Pudens actually reproached me with being poor, a charge which is welcome to a philosopher and one that he may glory in. For poverty has long been the handmaid of philosophy; frugal and sober, she is strong in her weakness and is greedy for naught save honour; the possession of her is a prophylactic against wealth, her mien is free from care, and her adornment simple; her counsels are beneficent, she puffs no man up with pride, she corrupts no man with passions beyond his control, she maddens no man with the lust for power, she neither desires nor can indulge in the pleasures of feasting and of love. These sins and their like are usually the nurslings of wealth. Count over all the greatest crimes recorded in the history of mankind, you will find no poor man among their guilty authors. On the other hand, it is rare to find wealthy men among the great figures of history. All those at whom we marvel for their great deeds were the nurslings of poverty from their very cradles, poverty that founded all cities in the days of old, poverty mother of all arts, witless of all sin, bestower of all glory, crowned with all honour among all the peoples of the world. Take the history of Greece: the justice of poverty is seen in [Aristides](), her benignity in [Phocion](), her force in

Epaminondas, her wisdom in Socrates, her eloquence in Homer. It was this same poverty that established the empire of the Roman people in its first beginnings, and even to this day Rome offers up thanksgivings for it to the immortal gods with libations poured from a wooden ladle and offerings borne in an earthen platter. If the judges sitting to try this case were Caius Fabricius, Cnaeus Scipio, Manius Curius, whose daughters on account of their poverty were given dowries from the public treasury and so went to their husbands bringing with them the honour of their houses and the wealth of the state; if Publicola, who drove out the Kings, or Agrippa, the healer of the people's strife, men whose funerals were on account of their poverty enriched by the gift of a few farthings per man from the whole Roman people; if Atilius Regulus, whose lands on account of his own poverty were cultivated at the public expense; if, in a word, all the heroes of the old Roman stock, consuls and censors and triumphant generals, were given a brief renewal of life and sent back to earth to give hearing to this case, would you dare in the presence of so many poor consuls to reproach a philosopher with poverty?

19. Perhaps Claudius Maximus seems to you to be a suitable person before whom to deride poverty, because he himself is in enjoyment of great wealth and enormous opulence. You are wrong, Aemilianus, you are wholly mistaken in your estimate of his character, if you take the bounty of his fortune rather than the sternness of his philosophy as the standard for your judgement and fail to realize that one, who holds so austere a creed and has so long endured military service, is more likely to befriend a moderate fortune with all its limitations than opulence with all its luxury, and holds that fortunes, like tunics, should be comfortable, not long. For even a tunic, if it be not carried high, but is allowed to drag, will entangle and trip the feet as badly as a cloak that hangs down in front. In everything that we employ for the needs of daily life, whatever exceeds the mean is superfluous and a burden rather than a help. So it is that excessive riches, like steering oars of too great weight and bulk, serve to sink the ship rather than to guide it; for their bulk is unprofitable and their superfluity a curse. I have noticed that of the wealthy themselves those win most praise who live quietly and in moderate comfort, concealing their actual resources, administering their great possessions without ostentation or pride and showing like poor folk under the disguise of their moderation. Now, if even the rich to some extent affect the outward form and semblance of poverty to give evidence of their moderation, why should we of slenderer means be ashamed of being poor not in appearance only but in reality?

20. I might even engage with you in controversy over the word poverty, urging that no man is poor who rejects the superfluous and has at his command all the necessities of life, which nature has ordained should be

exceedingly small. For he who desires least will possess most, inasmuch as he who wants but little will have all he wants. The measure of wealth ought therefore not to be the possession of lands and investments, but the very soul of man. For if avarice make him continually in need of some fresh acquisition and insatiable in his lust for gain, not even mountains of gold will bring him satisfaction, but he will always be begging for more that he may increase what he already possesses. That is *the* genuine admission of poverty. For every desire for fresh acquisition springs from the consciousness of want, and it matters little how large your possessions are if they are too small for *you*. Philus had a far smaller household than Laelius, Laelius than Scipio, Scipio than Crassus the Rich, and yet not even Crassus had as much as he wanted; and so, though he surpassed all others in wealth, he was himself surpassed by his own avarice and seemed rich to all save himself. On the other hand, the philosophers of whom I have spoken wanted nothing beyond what was at their disposal, and, thanks to the harmony existing between their desires and their resources, they were deservedly rich and happy. For poverty consists in the need for fresh acquisition, wealth in the satisfaction springing from the absence of needs. For the badge of penury is desire, the badge of wealth contempt. Therefore, Aemilianus, if you wish me to be regarded as poor, you must first prove that I am avaricious. But if my soul lacks nothing, I care little how much of the goods of this world be lacking to me; for it is no honour to possess them and no reproach to lack them.

21. But let us suppose it to be otherwise. Suppose that I am poor, because fortune has grudged me riches, because my guardian, as often happens, misappropriated my inheritance, some enemy robbed me, or my father left me nothing. Is it just to reproach a man for that which is regarded as no reproach to the animal kingdom, to the eagle, to the bull, to the lion? If the horse be strong in the possession of his peculiar excellences, if he is pleasant to ride and swift in his paces, no one rebukes him for the poverty of his food. Must you then reproach me, not for any scandalous word or deed, but simply because I live in a small house, possess an unusually small number of slaves, subsist on unusually light diet, wear unusually light clothing, and make unusually small purchases of food? Yet however scanty my service, food, and raiment may seem to you, I on the contrary regard them as ample and even excessive. Indeed I am desirous of still further reducing them, since the less I have to distract me the happier I shall be. For the soul, like the body, goes lightly clad when in good health; weakness wraps itself up, and it is a sure sign of infirmity to have many wants. We live, just as we swim, all the better for being but lightly burdened. For in this stormy life as on the stormy ocean heavy things sink us and light things buoy us up. It is in this respect, I find, that the gods more especially surpass men, namely that they lack nothing:

wherefore he of mankind whose needs are smallest is most like unto the gods.

22. I therefore regarded it as a compliment when to insult me you asserted that my whole household consisted of a wallet and a staff. Would that my spirit were made of such stern stuff as to permit me to dispense with all this furniture and worthily to carry that equipment for which Crates sacrificed all his wealth! Crates, I tell you, though I doubt if you will believe me, Aemilianus, was a man of great wealth and honour among the nobility of Thebes; but for love of this habit, which you cast in my face as a crime, he gave his large and luxurious household to his fellow citizens, resigned his troops of slaves for solitude, so contemned the countless trees of his rich orchards as to be content with one staff, exchanged his elegant villas for one small wallet, which, when he had fully appreciated its utility, he even praised in song by diverting from their original meaning certain lines of Homer in which he extols the island of Crete. I will quote the first lines, that you may not think this a mere invention of mine designed to meet the needs of my own case:

*There is a town named Wallet in the midst
Of smoke that's dark as wine.*

The lines which follow are so wonderful, that had you read them you would envy me my wallet even more than you envy me my marriage with Pudentilla. You reproach philosophers for their staff and wallet. You might as well reproach cavalry for their trappings, infantry for their shields, standard-bearers for their banners, triumphant generals for their chariots drawn by four white horses and their cloaks embroidered with palm-leaves. The staff and wallet are not, it is true, carried by the Platonic philosophers, but are the badges of the Cynic school. To Diogenes and Antisthenes they were what the crown is to the king, the cloak of purple to the general, the cowl to the priest, the trumpet to the augur. Indeed the Cynic Diogenes, when he disputed with Alexander the Great, as to which of the two was the true king, boasted of his staff as the true sceptre. The unconquered Hercules himself, since you despise my instances as drawn from mere mendicancy, Hercules that roamed the whole world, exterminated monsters, and conquered races, god though he was, had but a skin for raiment and a staff for company in the days when he wandered through the earth. And yet but a brief while afterwards he was admitted to heaven as a reward for his virtue.

23. But if you despise these examples and challenge me, not to plead my case, but to enter into a discussion of the amount of my fortune, to put an end to your ignorance on this point, if it exists, I acknowledge that my father left my brother and myself a little under 2,000,000 sesterces—a sum on which my lengthy travels, continual studies, and frequent generosity have made

considerable inroads. For I have often assisted my friends and have shown substantial gratitude to many of my instructors, on more than one occasion going so far as to provide dowries for their daughters. Nay, I should not have hesitated to expend every farthing of my patrimony, if so I might acquire, what is far better, a contempt for it. But as for you, Aemilianus, and ignorant boors of your kidney, in your case the fortune makes the man. You are like barren and blasted trees that produce no fruit, but are valued only for the timber that their trunks contain. But I beg you, Aemilianus, in future to abstain from reviling any one for their poverty, since you yourself used, after waiting for some seasonable shower to soften the ground, to expend three days in ploughing single-handed, with the aid of one wretched ass, that miserable farm at Zarath, which was all your father left you. It is only recently that fortune has smiled on you in the shape of wholly undeserved inheritances which have fallen to you by the frequent deaths of relatives, deaths to which, far more than to your hideous face, you owe your nickname of Charon.

24. As to my birthplace, you assert that my writings prove it to lie right on the marches of Numidia and Gaetulia, for I publicly described myself as half Numidian, half Gaetulian in a discourse delivered in the presence of that most distinguished citizen [Lollianus Avitus](). I do not see that I have any more reason to be ashamed of that than had the elder Cyrus for being of mixed descent, half Mede, half Persian. A man's birthplace is of no importance, it is his character that matters. We must consider not in what part of the world, but with what purpose he set out to live his life. Vendors of wine and cabbages are permitted to enhance the value of their wares by advertising the excellence of the soil whence they spring, as for instance with the wine of Thasos and the cabbages of Phlius. For those products of the soil are wonderfully improved in flavour by the fertility of the district which produces them, the moistness of the climate, the mildness of the winds, the warmth of the sun, and the richness of the soil. But in the case of man, the soul enters the tenement of the body from without. What, then, can such circumstances as these add to or take away from his virtues or his vices? Has there ever been a time or place in which a race has not produced a variety of intellects, although some races seem stupider and some wiser than others? The Scythians are the stupidest of men, and yet the wise [Anacharsis]() was a Scyth. The Athenians are shrewd, and yet the Athenian [Meletides]() was a fool. I say this not because I am ashamed of my country, since even in the time of [Syphax]() we were a township. When he was conquered we were transferred by the gift of the Roman people to the dominion of King Masinissa, and finally as the result of a settlement of veteran soldiers, our second founders, we have become a colony of the highest distinction. In this same colony my father attained to the post of *[duumvir]()* and became the foremost citizen of the place, after filling all the municipal offices of honour. I myself, immediately

after my first entry into the municipal senate, succeeded to my father's position in the community, and, as I hope, am in no ways a degenerate successor, but receive like honour and esteem for my maintenance of the dignity of my position. Why do I mention this? That you, Aemilianus, may be less angry with me in future and may more readily pardon me for having been negligent enough not to select your 'Attic' Zarath for my birthplace.

25. Are you not ashamed to produce such accusations with such violence before such a judge, to bring forward frivolous and self-contradictory accusations, and then in the same breath to blame me on both charges at once? Is it not a sheer contradiction to object to my wallet and staff on the ground of austerity, to my poems and mirror on the ground of undue levity; to accuse me of parsimony for having only one slave, and of extravagance in having three; to denounce me for my Greek eloquence and my barbarian birth? Awake from your slumber and remember that you are speaking before Claudius Maximus, a man of stern character, burdened with the business of the whole province. Cease, I say, to bring forward these empty slanders. Prove your indictment, prove that I am guilty of ghastly crimes, detestable sorceries, and black art-magic. Why is it that the strength of your speech lies in mere noise, while it is weak and flabby in point of facts?

I will now deal with the actual charge of magic. You spared no violence in fanning the flame of hatred against me. But you have disappointed all men's expectations by your old wives' fables, and the fire kindled by your accusations has burned itself away. I ask you, Maximus, have you ever seen fire spring up among the stubble, crackling sharply, blazing wide and spreading fast, but soon exhausting its flimsy fuel, dying fast away, leaving not a wrack behind? So they have kindled their accusation with abuse and fanned it with words, but it lacks the fuel of facts and, your verdict once given, is destined to leave not a wrack of calumny behind. The whole of Aemilianus' calumnious accusation was centred in the charge of magic. I should therefore like to ask his most learned advocates how, precisely, they would define a magician. If what I read in a large number of authors be true, namely, that magician is the Persian word for priest, what is there criminal in being a priest and having due knowledge, science, and skill in all ceremonial law, sacrificial duties, and the binding rules of religion, at least if magic consists in that which Plato sets forth in his description of the methods employed by the Persians in the education of their young princes? I remember the very words of that divine philosopher. Let me recall them to your memory, Maximus: 'When the boy has reached the age of fourteen he is handed over to the care of men known as the Royal Masters. They are four in number, and are chosen as being the best of the elders of Persia, one the wisest, another the justest, a third the most temperate, a fourth the bravest. And one of these teaches the boy the magic of Zoroaster the son of

Oromazes; and this magic is no other than the worship of the gods. He also teaches him the arts of kingship.'

26. Do you hear, you who so rashly accuse the art of magic? It is an art acceptable to the immortal gods, full of all knowledge of worship and of prayer, full of piety and wisdom in things divine, full of honour and glory since the day when Zoroaster and Oromazes established it, high-priestess of the powers of heaven. Nay, it is one of the first elements of princely instruction, nor do they lightly admit any chance person to be a magician, any more than they would admit him to be a king. Plato—if I may quote him again—in another passage dealing with a certain Zalmoxis, a Thracian and also a master of this art, has written that 'magical charms are merely beautiful words'. If that is so, why should I be forbidden to learn the fair words of Zalmoxis or the priestly lore of Zoroaster? But if these accusers of mine, after the fashion of the common herd, define a magician as one who by communion of speech with the immortal gods has power to do all the marvels that he will, through a strange power of incantation, I really wonder that they are not afraid to attack one whom they acknowledge to be so powerful. For it is impossible to guard against such a mysterious and divine power. Against other dangers we may take adequate precautions. He who summons a murderer before the judge comes into court with an escort of friends; he who denounces a poisoner is unusually careful as to what he eats; he who accuses a thief sets a guard over his possessions. But for the man who exposes a magician, credited with such awful powers, to the danger of a capital sentence, how can escort or precaution or watchmen save him from unforeseen and inevitable disaster? Nothing can save him, and therefore the man who believes in the truth of such a charge as this is certainly the last person in the world who should bring such an accusation.

27. But it is a common and general error of the uninitiated to bring the following accusations against philosophers. Some of them think that those who explore the origins and elements of material things are irreligious, and assert that they deny the existence of the gods. Take, for instance, the cases of Anaxagoras, Leucippus, Democritus, and Epicurus, and other natural philosophers. Others call those magicians who bestow unusual care on the investigation of the workings of providence and unusual devotion on their worship of the gods, as though, forsooth, they knew *how* to perform everything that they know actually to *be* performed. So Epimenides, Orpheus, Pythagoras, and Ostanes were regarded as magicians, while a similar suspicion attached to the 'purifications' of Empedocles, the 'demon' of Socrates and the 'good' of Plato. I congratulate myself therefore on being admitted to such distinguished company.

I fear, however, Maximus, that you may regard the empty, ridiculous and childish[9] fictions which my opponents have advanced in support of their case as serious charges merely because they have been put forward. 'Why,' says my accuser, 'have you sought out particular kinds of fish?' Why should not a philosopher be permitted to do for the satisfaction of his desire for knowledge what the *gourmand*, is permitted to do for the satisfaction of his gluttony? 'What,' he asks, 'induced a free woman to marry you after thirteen years of widowhood?' 'Surely,' I answer, 'it is more remarkable that she should have remained a widow so long.' 'Why, before she married you, did she express certain opinions in a letter?' 'Is it reasonable,' I ask, 'to demand of any one the reasons of another person's private opinions?' 'But,' he goes on, 'although she was your senior in years, she did not despise your youth.' Surely this simply serves to show that there was no need of magic to induce a woman to marry a man, or a widow to wed a bachelor some years her junior. There are more charges equally frivolous. 'Apuleius,' he persists, 'keeps a mysterious object in his house which he worships with veneration.' Surely it would be a worse offence to have nothing to worship at all. 'A boy fell to the ground in Apuleius' presence.' What if a young man or even an old man had fallen in my presence through a sudden stroke of disease or merely owing to the slipperiness of the ground? Do you really think to prove your charge of magic by such arguments as these; the fall of a wretched boy, my marriage to my wife, my purchases of fish?

28. I should run but small risk if I were to content myself with what I have already said and begin my peroration. But since as a result of the length at which my accusers spoke, the water-clock still allows me plenty of time, let us, if there is no objection, consider the charges in detail. I will deny none of them, be they true or false. I will assume their truth, that this great crowd, which has gathered from all directions to hear this case, may clearly understand not only that no true incrimination can be brought against philosophers, but that not even any false charge can be fabricated against them, which—such is their confidence in their innocence—they will not be prepared to admit and to defend, even though it be in their power to deny it. I will therefore begin by refuting their arguments, and will prove that they have nothing to do with magic. Next I will show that even on the assumption of my being the most consummate magician, I have never given cause or occasion for conviction of any evil practice. I will also deal with the lies with which they have endeavoured to arouse hostility against me, with their misquotation and misinterpretation of my wife's letters, and with my marriage with Pudentilla, whom, as I will proceed to prove, I married for love and not for money. This marriage of ours caused frightful annoyance and distress to Aemilianus. Hence springs all the anger, frenzy, and raving madness that he has shown in the conduct of this accusation. If I succeed in making all these points abundantly clear and obvious, I shall then appeal to you, Claudius Maximus, and to all here present to bear me out, that the boy Sicinius Pudens, my step-son, through whom and with whose consent his

uncle now accuses me, was quite recently stolen from my charge after the death of Pontianus his brother, who was as much his superior in character as in years, and that he was fiercely embittered against myself and his mother through no fault of mine: that he abandoned his study of the liberal arts and cast off all restraint, and—thanks to the education afforded him by this villainous accusation—is more likely to resemble his uncle Aemilianus than his brother Pontianus.

29. I will now, as I promised, take Aemilianus' ravings one by one, beginning with that charge which you must have noticed was given the place of honour in the accuser's speech, as his most effective method of exciting suspicion against me as a sorcerer, the charge that I had sought to purchase certain kinds of fish from some fishermen. Which of these two points is of the slightest value as affording suspicion of sorcery? That fishermen sought to procure me the fish? Would you have me entrust such a task to gold-embroiderers or carpenters, and, to avoid your calumnies, make them change their trades so that the carpenter would net me the fish, and the fisherman take his place and hew his timber? Or did you infer that the fish were wanted for evil purposes because I paid to get them? I presume, if I had wanted them for a dinner-party, I should have got them for nothing. Why do not you go farther and accuse me on many similar grounds? I have often bought wine and vegetables, fruit and bread. The principles laid down by you would involve the starvation of all purveyors of dainties. Who will ever venture to purchase food from them, if it be decided that all provisions for which money is given are wanted not for food but for sorcery? But if there is nothing in all this that can give rise to suspicion, neither the payment of the fishermen to ply their usual trade, to wit, the capture of fish—I may point out that the prosecution never produced any of these fishermen, who are, as a matter of fact, wholly creatures of their imagination—nor the purchase of a common article of sale—the prosecution have never stated the amount paid, for fear that if they mentioned a small sum, it would be regarded as trivial, or if they mentioned a large sum it would fail to win belief,—if, I say, there is no cause for suspicion on any of these grounds, I would ask Aemilianus to tell me what, failing these, induced them to accuse me of magic.

30. 'You seek to purchase fish,' says he. I will not deny it. But, I ask you, is any one who does that a magician? No more, in my opinion, than if I should seek to purchase hares or boar's flesh or fatted capons. Or is there something mysterious in fish and fish alone, hidden from all save sorcerers only? If you know what it is, clearly you are a magician. If you do not know, you must confess that you are bringing an accusation of the nature of which you are entirely ignorant. To think that you should be so ignorant not only of all literature, but even of popular tales, that you cannot even invent charges that

will have some show of plausibility! For of what use for the kindling of love is an unfeeling chilly creature like a fish, or indeed anything else drawn from the sea, unless indeed you propose to bring forward in support of your lie the legend that Venus was born from the sea? I beg you to listen to me, Tannonius Pudens, that you may learn the extent of the ignorance which you have shown by accepting the possession of a fish as a proof of sorcery. If you had read your Vergil, you would certainly have known that very different things are sought for this purpose. He, as far as I recollect, mentions 'soft garlands' and 'rich herbs and 'male incense' and 'threads of diverse hues', and, in addition to these, 'brittle laurel,' 'clay to be hardened,' and 'wax to be melted in the fire'. There are also the objects mentioned by him in a more serious poem.

Rank herbs are sought, with milky venom dark
By brazen sickles under moonlight mown;
Sought also is that wondrous talisman,
Torn from the forehead of the foal at birth
Ere yet its dam could snatch it.

But you who take such exception to fish attribute far different instruments to magicians, charms not to be torn from new-born foreheads, but to be cut from scaly backs; not to be plucked from the fields of earth, but to be drawn up from the deep fields of ocean; not to be mowed with sickles, but to be caught on hooks. Finally, when he is speaking of the black art, Vergil mentions poison, you produce an *entrée*; he mentions herbs and young shoots, you talk of scales and bones; he crops the meadow, you search the waves. I would also have quoted for your benefit similar passages from Theocritus with many others from Homer and Orpheus, from the comic and tragic poets and from the historians, had I not noticed ere now that you were unable to read Pudentilla's letter which was written in Greek. I will, therefore, do no more than cite one Latin poet. Those who have read Laevius[10] will recognize the lines.

Love-charms the warlocks seek through all the world:
The 'lover's knot' they try, the magic wheel,
Ribbons and, nails and roots and herbs and shoots,
The two-tailed lizard that draws on to love,[11]
And eke the charm that glads the whinnying mare.

31. You would have made out a far more plausible case by pretending that I made use of such things instead of fish, if only you had possessed the slightest erudition. For the belief in the use of these things is so widespread that you might have been believed. But of what use are fish save to be cooked and eaten at meals? In magic they seem to me to be absolutely useless. I will

tell you why I think so. Many hold Pythagoras to have been a pupil of Zoroaster, and, like him, to have been skilled in magic. And yet it is recorded that once near Metapontum, on the shores of Italy, his home, which his influence had converted into a second Greece, he noticed certain fishermen draw up their net. He offered to buy whatever it might contain, and after depositing the price ordered all the fish caught in meshes of the net to be released and thrown back into the sea. He would assuredly never have allowed them to slip from his possession had he known them to possess any valuable magical properties. For being a man of abnormal learning, and a great admirer of the men of old, he remembered that Homer, a poet of manifold or, rather I should say, absolute knowledge of all that may be known, spoke of the power of all the drugs that earth produces, but made no mention of the sea, when speaking of a certain witch, he wrote the line:

All drugs, that wide earth nourishes, she knew.

Similarly in another passage he says:

Earth the grain-giver
Yields up to her its store of drugs, whereof
Many be healing, mingled in the cup,
And many baneful.

But never in the works of Homer did Proteus anoint his face nor Ulysses his magic trench, nor Aeolus his windbags, nor Helen her mixing bowl, nor Circe her cup, nor Venus her girdle, with any charm drawn from the sea or its inhabitants. You alone within the memory of man have been found to sweep as it were by some convulsion of nature all the powers of herbs and roots and young shoots and small pebbles from their hilltops into the sea, and there confine them in the entrails of fish. And so whereas sorcerers at their rites used to call on Mercury the giver of oracles, Venus that lures the soul, the moon that knows the mystery of the night, and Trivia the mistress of the shades, you will transfer Neptune, with Salacia and Portumnus and all the company of Nereids from the cold tides of the sea to the burning tides of love.

32. I have given my reasons for refusing to believe that magicians and fish have anything to do with one another. But now, if it please you, we will assume with Aemilianus that fish are useful for making magical charms as well as for their usual purposes. But does that prove that whoever acquires fish is *ipso facto* a magician? On those lines it might be urged that whoever acquires a sloop is a pirate, whoever acquires a crowbar a burglar, whoever acquires a sword an assassin. You will say that there is nothing in the world, however harmless, that may not be put to some bad use, nothing so cheerful that it may not be given a gloomy meaning. And yet we do not on that

account put a bad interpretation on everything, as though, for instance, you should hold that incense, cassia, myrrh, and similar other scents are purchased solely for the purpose of funerals; whereas they are also used for sacrifice and medicine. But on the lines of your argument you must believe that even the comrades of Menelaus were magicians; for they, according to the great poet, averted starvation at the isle of Pharos by their use of curved fish-hooks. Nay, you will class in the same category of sorcerers seamews, dolphins, and the lobster; *gourmands* also, who sink whole fortunes[12] in the sums they pay to fishermen; and fishermen themselves, who by their art capture all manner of fish. 'But what do you want fish for?' you insist. I feel myself under no necessity to tell you, and refuse to do so. But I challenge you to prove unsupported that I bought them for the purpose you assert; as though I had bought hellebore or hemlock or opium or any other of those drugs, the moderate use of which is salutary, although they are deadly when given with other substances or in too large quantities. Who would endure it if you made this a ground for accusing me of being a poisoner, merely because those drugs are capable of killing a man?

33. However, let us see what these fish were, fish so necessary for my possession and so hard to find, that they were well worth the price I paid for their acquisition. They have mentioned no more than three. To one they gave a false name; as regards the other two they lied. The name was false, for they asserted that the fish was a sea-hare, whereas it was quite another fish, which Themison, my servant, who knows something of medicine, as you heard from his own lips, bought of his own suggestion for me to inspect. For, as a matter of fact, he has not as yet ever come across a sea-hare. But I admit that I search for other kinds of fish as well, and have commissioned not only fishermen but private friends to search for all the rarest kinds of fish, begging them either to describe the appearance of the fish or to send it me, if possible, alive, or, failing that, dead. Why I do so I will soon make clear. My accusers *lied*—and very cunning they thought themselves—when they closed their false accusation by pretending that I had sought for two sea-beasts known by gross names. That fellow Tannonius wished to indicate the nature of the obscenity, but failed, matchless pleader that he is, owing to his inability to speak. After long hesitation he indicated the name of one of them by means of some clumsy and disgusting circumlocution. The other he found impossible to describe with decency, and evaded the difficulty by turning to my works and quoting a certain passage from them in which I described the attitude of a statue of Venus.

34. He also with that lofty puritanism which characterizes him, reproached me for not being ashamed to describe foul things in noble language. I might justly retort on him that, though he openly professes the study of eloquence, that stammering voice of his often gives utterance to noble things so basely

as to defile them, and that frequently, when what he has to say presents not the slightest difficulty, he begins to stutter or even becomes utterly tongue-tied. Come now! Suppose I had said nothing about the statue of Venus, nor used the phrase which was of such service to you, what words would you have found to frame a charge, which is as suited to your stupidity as to your powers of speech? I ask you, is there anything more idiotic than the inference that, because the names of two things resemble each other, the things themselves are identical? Or did you think it a particularly clever invention on your part to pretend that I had sought out these two fish for the purpose of using them as magical charms? Remember that it is as absurd an argument to say that these sea-creatures with gross names were sought for gross purposes, as to say that the sea-comb is sought for the adornment of the hair, the fish named sea-hawk to catch birds, the fish named the little boar for the hunting of boars, or the sea-skull to raise the dead. My reply to these lying fabrications, which are as stupid as they are absurd, is that I have never attempted to acquire these playthings of the sea, these tiny trifles of the shore, either gratis or for money.

35. Further, I reply that you were quite ignorant of the nature of the objects which you pretended that I sought to acquire. For these worthless fish you mention can be found on any shore in heaps and multitudes, and are cast up on dry land by the merest ripple without any need for human agency. Why do you not say that at the same time I commissioned large numbers of fishermen to secure for me at a price striped sea-shells from the shore, smooth pebbles, crabs' claws, sea-urchins' husks, the tentacles of cuttlefish, shingle, straws, cordage, not to mention[13] worm-eaten oyster-shells, moss, and seaweed, and all the flotsam of the sea that the winds drive, or the salt wave casts up, or the storm sweeps back, or the calm leaves high and dry all along our shores? For their names are no less suitable than those I mentioned above for the purpose of awakening suspicions. You have said that certain objects drawn from the sea have a certain value for gross purposes on account of the similarity of their names. On this analogy why should not a stone be good for diseases of the bladder, a shell for the making of a will, a crab for a cancer, seaweed for an ague? Really, Claudius Maximus, in listening to these appallingly long-winded accusations to their very close you have shown a patience that is excessive and a kindness which is too long-suffering. For my part when they uttered these charges of theirs, as though they were serious and cogent, while I laughed at their stupidity, I marvelled at your patience.

36. However, since he takes so much interest in my affairs, I will now tell Aemilianus why I have examined so many fishes already and why I am unwilling to remain in ignorance of some I have not yet seen. Although he is in the decline of life and suffering from senile decay, let him, if he will,

acquire some learning even at the eleventh hour. Let him read the works of the philosophers of old, that now at any rate he may learn that I am not the first ichthyologist, but follow in the steps of authors, centuries my seniors, such as Aristotle, Theophrastus, Eudemus, Lycon, and the other successors of Plato, who have left many books on the generation, life, parts and differences of animals. It is a good thing, Maximus, that this case is being tried before a scholar like yourself, who have read Aristotle's numerous volumes 'on the generation, the anatomy, the history of animals', together with his numberless 'Problems' and works by others of his school, treating of various subjects of this kind. If it is an honour and glory to them that they should have put on record the results of their careful researches, why should it be disgraceful to me to attempt the like task, especially since I shall attempt to write on those subjects both in Greek and Latin and in a more concise and systematic manner, and shall strive either to make good omissions or remedy mistakes in all these authors? I beg of you, if you think it worth while, to permit the reading of extracts from my 'magic' works, that Aemilianus may learn that my sedulous researches and inquiries have a wider range than he thinks. Bring a volume of my Greek works—some of my friends who are interested in questions of natural history may perhaps have them with them in court—take by preference one of those dealing with problems of natural philosophy, and from among those that volume in particular which treats of the race of fish. While he is looking for the book, I will tell you a story which has some relevance to this case.

37. The poet Sophocles, the rival and survivor of Euripides—for he lived to extreme old age—on being accused by his own son of insanity on the ground that the advance of age had destroyed his wits, is said to have produced that matchless tragedy, his *Oedipus Coloneus*, on which he happened to be engaged at the time, and to have read it aloud to the jury without adding another word in his defence, except that he bade them without hesitation to condemn him as insane if an old man's poetry displeased them. At that point—so I have read—the jury rose to their feet as one man to show their admiration of so great a poet, and praised him marvellously both for the shrewdness of his argument and for the eloquence of his tragic verse. And indeed they were not far off unanimously condemning the accuser as the madman instead.

Have you found the book? Thank you. Let us try now whether what I write may serve me in good stead in a law-court. Read a few lines at the beginning, then some details concerning the fish. And do you while he reads stop the water-clock. (*A passage from the book is read.*)

38. You hear, Maximus. You have doubtless frequently read the like in the works of ancient philosophers. Remember too that these volumes of mine describe fishes only, distinguishing those that spring from the union of the sexes from those which are spontaneously generated from the mud,

discussing how often and at what periods of the year the males and females of each species come together, setting forth the distinction established by nature between those of them who are viviparous and those who are oviparous—for thus I translate the Greek phrases ζῳοτόκα and ᾠοτόκα—together with the causes of this distinction and the organic differences by which it is characterized, in a word—for I would not weary you by discussing all the different methods of generation in animals—treating of the distinguishing marks of species, their various manners of life, the difference of their members and ages, with many other points necessary for the man of science but out of place in a law-court. I will ask that a few of my Latin writings dealing with the same science may be read, in which you will notice some rare pieces of knowledge and names but little known to the Romans; indeed they have never been produced before to-day, but yet, thanks to my toil and study they have been so translated from the Greek, that in spite of their strangeness they are none the less of Latin mintage. Do you deny this, Aemilianus? If so, let your advocates tell me in what Latin author they have ever before read such words as those which I will cause to be recited to you. I will mention only aquatic animals, nor will I make any reference to other animals save in connexion with the characteristics which distinguish them from aquatic creatures. Listen then to what I say. You will cry out at me saying that I am giving you a list of magic names such as are used in Egyptian or Babylonian rites. Σελάχεια μαλάχεια μαλακόστρακα χονδράκανθα ὀστρακόδερμα καρχαρόδοντα ἀμφίβια λεπιδωτὰ φολιδωτὰ δερμόπτερα στεγανόποδα μονήρη συναγελαστικά. I might continue the list, but it is not worth wasting time over such trifles, and I need time to deal with other charges. Meanwhile read out my translation into Latin of the few names I have just given you. (*The translation is read. The Latin names are lost.*)

39. What think you? Is it disgraceful for a philosopher who is no rude and unlearned person of the reckless Cynic type, but who remembers that he is a disciple of Plato, is it disgraceful for such an one to know and care for such learning or to be ignorant and indifferent? to know how far such things reveal the workings of providence, or to swallow all the tales his father and mother told him of the immortal gods? Quintus Ennius wrote a poem on dainties: he there enumerates countless species of fish, which of course he had carefully studied. I remember a few lines and will recite them:

Clipea's sea-weasels are of all the best,
For 'mice' the place is Aenus; oysters rough
In greatest plenty from Abydos come.
The sea-comb's found at Mitylene and
Ambracian Charadrus, and I praise
Brundisian sargus: take him, if he's big.
Know that Tarentum's small sea-boar is prime;

The sword-fish at Surrentum thou shouldst buy;
Blue fish at Cumae. What! have I passed by
Scarus? the brain of Jove is not less sweet.
You catch them large and good off Nestor's home.
Have I passed by the black-tail and the 'thrush',
The sea-merle and the shadow of the sea?
Best to Corcyra go for cuttlefish,
For the acarnè and the fat sea-skull
The purple-fish, the little murex too,
Mice of the sea and the sea-urchin sweet.

He glorified many fish in other verses, stating where each was to be found and whether they were best fried or stewed, and yet he is not blamed for it by the learned. Spare then to blame me, who describe things known to few under elegant and appropriate names both in Greek and Latin.

40. Enough of this! I call your attention to another point. What if I take such interest and possess such skill in medicine as to search for certain remedies in fish? For assuredly as nature with impartial munificence has distributed and implanted many remedies throughout all other created things, so also similar remedies are to be found in fish. Now, do you think it more the business of a magician than of a doctor, or indeed of a philosopher, to know and seek out remedies? For the philosopher will use them not to win money for his purse, but to give assistance to his fellow men. The doctors of old indeed knew how to cure wounds by magic song, as Homer, the most reliable of all the writers of antiquity, tells us, making the blood of Ulysses to be stayed by a chant as it gushed forth from a wound. Now nothing that is done to save life can be matter for accusation. 'But,' says my adversary, 'for what purpose save evil did you dissect the fish brought you by your servant Themison?' As if I had not told you just now that I write treatises on the organs of all kind of animals, describing the place, number and purpose of their various parts, diligently investigating Aristotle's works on anatomy and adding to them where necessary. I am, therefore, greatly surprised that you are only aware of my having inspected one small fish, although I have actually inspected a very large number under all circumstances wherever I might find them, and have, moreover, made no secret of my researches, but conducted them openly before all the world, so that the merest stranger may, if it please him, stand by and observe me. In this I follow the instruction of my masters, who assert that a free man of free spirit should as far as possible wear his thoughts upon his face. Indeed I actually showed this small fish, which you call a sea-hare, to many who stood by. I do not yet know what name to call it[14] without closer research, since in spite of its rarity and most remarkable characteristics I do not find it described by any of the ancient philosophers. This fish is, as far as my knowledge extends, unique in one respect, for it

contains twelve bones resembling the knuckle-bones of a sucking-pig, linked together like a chain in its belly. Apart from this it is boneless. Had Aristotle known this, Aristotle who records as a most remarkable phenomenon the fact that the fish known as the small sea-ass alone of all fishes has its diminutive heart placed in its stomach, he would assuredly have mentioned the fact.

41. 'You dissected a fish,' says he. Who can call this a crime in a philosopher which would be no crime in a butcher or cook? 'You dissected a fish.' Perhaps you object to the fact that it was raw. You would not regard it as criminal if I had explored its stomach and cut up its delicate liver after it was cooked, as you teach the boy Sicinius Pudens to do with his own fish at meals. And yet it is a greater crime for a philosopher to eat fish than to inspect them. Are augurs to be allowed to explore the livers of victims and may not a philosopher look at them too, a philosopher who knows that he can draw omens from every animal, that he is the high-priest of every god? Do you bring that as a reproach against me which is one of the reasons for the admiration with which Maximus and myself regard Aristotle? Unless you drive his works from the libraries and snatch them from the hands of students you cannot accuse me. But enough! I have said almost more on this subject than I ought.

See, too, how they contradict themselves. They say that I sought my wife in marriage with the help of the black art and charms drawn from the sea at the very time when they acknowledge me to have been in the midmost mountains of Gaetulia, where, I suppose, Deucalion's deluge has made it possible to find fish! I am, however, glad that they do not know that I have read Theophrastus' 'On beasts that bite and sting' and Nicander 'On the bites of wild animals'; otherwise they would have accused me of poisoning as well! As a matter of fact I have acquired a knowledge of these subjects thanks to my reading of Aristotle and my desire to emulate him. I owe something also to the advice of my master Plato, who says that those who make such investigations as these 'pursue a delightful form of amusement which they will never regret'.

42. Since I have sufficiently cleared up this business of the fish, listen to another of their inventions equally stupid, but much more extravagant and far more wicked. They themselves knew that their argument about the fish was futile and bound to fail. They realized, moreover, its strange absurdity (for who ever heard of fish being scaled and boned for dark purposes of magic?), they realized that it would be better for their fictions to deal with things of more common report, which have ere now been believed. And so they devised the following fiction which does at least fall within the limits of popular credence and rumour. They asserted that I had taken a boy apart to a secret place with a small altar and a lantern and only a few accomplices as

witnesses, and there so bewitched him with a magical incantation that he fell in the very spot where I pronounced the charm, and on being awakened was found to be out of his wits. They did not dare to go any further with the lie. To complete their story they should have added that the boy uttered many prophecies. For this we know is the prize of magical incantations, namely divination and prophecy. And this miracle in the case of boys is confirmed not only by vulgar opinion but by the authority of learned men. I remember reading various relations of the kind in the philosopher Varro, a writer of the highest learning and erudition, but there was the following story in particular. Inquiry was being made at Tralles by means of magic into the probable issue of the Mithridatic war, and a boy who was gazing at an image of Mercury reflected in a bowl of water foretold the future in a hundred and sixty lines of verse. He records also that Fabius, having lost five hundred denarii, came to consult Nigidius; the latter by means of incantations inspired certain boys so that they were able to indicate to him where a pot containing a certain portion of the money had been hidden in the ground, and how the remainder had been dispersed, one denarius having found its way into the possession of Marcus Cato the philosopher. This coin Cato acknowledged he had received from a certain lackey as a contribution to the treasury of Apollo.

43. I have read this and the like concerning boys and art-magic in several authors, but I am in doubt whether to admit the truth of such stories or no, although I believe Plato when he asserts that there are certain divine powers holding a position and possessing a character midway between gods and men, and that all divination and the miracles of magicians are controlled by them. Moreover it is my own personal opinion that the human soul, especially when it is young and unsophisticated, may by the allurement of music or the soothing influence of sweet smells be lulled into slumber and banished into oblivion of its surroundings so that, as all consciousness of the body fades from the memory, it returns and is reduced to its primal nature, which is in truth immortal and divine; and thus, as it were in a kind of slumber, it may predict the future. But howsoever these things may be, if any faith is to be put in them, the prophetic boy must, as far as I can understand, be fair and unblemished in body, shrewd of wit and ready of speech, so that a worthy and fair shrine may be provided for the divine indwelling power— if indeed such a power does enter into the boy's body—or that the boy's mind when wakened may quickly apply itself to its inherent powers of divination, find them ready to its use and reproduce their promptings undulled and unimpaired by any loss of memory. For, as Pythagoras said, not every kind of wood is fit to be carved into the likeness of Mercury. If that be so, tell me who was that healthy, unblemished, intelligent, handsome boy whom I deemed worthy of initiation into such mysteries by the power of my spells. As a matter of fact, Thallus, whom you mentioned, needs a doctor rather than a magician. For the poor wretch is such a victim to epilepsy that

he frequently has fits twice or thrice in one day without the need for any incantations, and exhausts all his limbs with his convulsions. His face is ulcerous, his head bruised in front and behind, his eyes are dull, his nostrils distended, his feet stumbling. He may claim to be the greatest of magicians in whose presence Thallus has remained for any considerable time upon his feet. For he is continually lying down, either a seizure or mere weariness[15] causing him to collapse.

44. Yet you say that it is my incantations that have overwhelmed him, simply because he has once chanced to have a fit in my presence. Many of his fellow servants, whose appearance as witnesses you have demanded, are present in court. They all can tell you why it is they spit upon Thallus, and why no one ventures to eat from the same dish with him or to drink from the same cup. But why do I speak of these slaves? You yourselves have eyes. Deny then, if you dare, that Thallus used to have fits of epilepsy long before I came to Oea, or that has frequently been shown to doctors. Let his fellow slaves who are in your service deny this: I will confess myself guilty of everything, if he has not long since been sent away into the country, far from the sight of all of them, to a distant farm, for fear he should infect the rest of the household. They cannot deny this to be the fact. For the same reason it is impossible for us to produce him here to-day. The whole of this accusation has been reckless and sudden, and it was only the day before yesterday that Aemilianus demanded that we should produce fifteen slaves before you. The fourteen living in the town are present to-day. Thallus only is absent owing to the fact that he has been banished to a place some hundred miles distant. However, we have sent a man to bring him here in a carriage. I ask you, Maximus, to question these fourteen slaves whom we have produced as to where the boy Thallus is and what is the state of his health; I ask you to question my accuser's slaves. They will not deny that this boy is of revolting appearance, that his body is rotten through and through with disease, that he is liable to fits, and is a barbarian and a clodhopper. This is indeed a handsome boy whom you have selected as one who might fairly be produced at the offering of sacrifice, whom one might touch upon the head and clothe in a fair white cloak in expectation of some prophetic reply from his lips. I only wish he were present. I would have entrusted him to your tender mercies, Aemilianus, and would be ready to hold him myself that you might question him. Here in open court before the judges he would have rolled his wild eyes upon you, he would have foamed at the mouth, spat in your face, drawn in his hands convulsively, shaken his head and fallen at last in a fit into your arms.

45. Here are fourteen slaves whom you bade me produce in court. Why do you refuse to question them? You want one epileptic boy who, you know as well as I, has long been absent from Oea. What clearer evidence of the

falseness of your accusations could be desired? Fourteen slaves are present, as you required; you ignore them. One young boy is absent: you concentrate your attack on him. What is it that you want? Suppose Thallus were present. Do you want to prove that he had a fit in my presence? Why, I myself admit it. You say that this was the result of incantation. I answer that the boy knows nothing about it, and that I can prove that it was not so. Even you will not deny that Thallus was epileptic. Why then attribute his fall to magic rather than disease? Was there anything improbable in his suffering that fate in *my* presence, which he has often suffered on other occasions in the presence of a number of persons? Nay, even supposing I had thought it a great achievement to cast an epileptic into a fit, why should I use charms when, as I am told by writers on natural history, the burning of the stone named *gagates* is an equally sure and easy proof of the disease? For its scent is commonly used as a test of the soundness or infirmity of slaves even in the slave-market. Again, the spinning of a potter's wheel will easily infect a man suffering from this disease with its own giddiness. For the sight of its rotations weakens his already feeble mind, and the potter is far more effective than the magician for casting epileptics into convulsions. You had no reason for demanding that I should produce these slaves. I have good reason for asking you to name those who witnessed that guilty ritual when I cast the moribund Thallus into one of his fits. The only witness you mention is that worthless boy, Sicinius Pudens, in whose name you accuse me. He says that he was present. His extreme youth is no reason why we should reject his sworn evidence, but the fact that he is one of my accusers *does* detract from his credibility. It would have been easier for you, Aemilianus, and your evidence would have carried much more weight, had you said that you were present at the rite and had been mad ever since, instead of entrusting the whole business to the evidence of boys as though it were a mere joke. A boy had a fit, a boy saw him. Was it also some boy that bewitched him?

46. At this point Tannonius Pudens, like the old hand he is, saw that this lie also was falling flat and was doomed to failure by the frowns and murmurs of the audience, and so, in order to check the suspicions of some of them by kindling fresh expectations, he said that he would produce other boys as well whom I had similarly bewitched. He thus passed to another line of accusation. I might ignore it, but I will go out of my way to challenge it as I have done with all the rest. I want those boys to be produced. I hear they have been bribed by the promise of their liberty to perjure themselves. But I say no more. Only produce them. I demand and insist, Tannonius Pudens, that you should fulfil your promise. Bring forward those boys in whose evidence you put your trust; produce them, name them. You may use the time allotted to my speech for the purpose. Speak, I say, Tannonius. Why are you silent? Why do you hesitate? Why look round? If *he* does not remember his instructions, or has forgotten his witnesses' names, do you at any rate,

Aemilianus, come forward and tell us what instructions you gave your advocate, and produce those boys. Why do you turn pale? Why are you silent? Is this the way to bring an accusation? Is this the way to indict a man on so serious a charge? Is it not rather an insult to so distinguished a citizen as Claudius Maximus, and a false and slanderous persecution of myself? However, if your representative has made a slip in his speech, and there are no such boys to produce, at any rate make some use of the fourteen whom I have brought into court. If you refuse, why did you demand the appearance of such a housefull?

47. You have demanded fifteen slaves to support an accusation of magic; how many would you be demanding if it were a charge of violence? The inference is that fifteen slaves know something, and that something is still a mystery. Or is it nothing mysterious and yet something connected with magic? You must admit one of these two alternatives: either the proceeding to which I admitted so many witnesses had nothing improper about it, or, if it had, it should not have been witnessed by so many. Now this magic of which you accuse me is, I am told, a crime in the eyes of the law, and was forbidden in remote antiquity by the [Twelve Tables](#) because in some incredible manner crops had been charmed away from one field to another. It is then as mysterious an art as it is loathly and horrible; it needs as a rule night-watches and concealing darkness, solitude absolute and murmured incantations, to hear which few free men are admitted, not to speak of slaves. And yet you will have it that there were fifteen slaves present on this occasion. Was it a marriage? or any other crowded ceremony? or a seasonable banquet? Fifteen slaves take part in a magic rite as though they had been created *quindecimvirs* for the performance of sacrifice! Is it likely that I should have permitted so large a number to be present on such an occasion, if they were too many to be accomplices? Fifteen free men form a borough, fifteen slaves a household, fifteen fettered serfs a chain-gang. Did I need such a crowd to help me by holding the lustral victims during the lengthy rite? No! the only victims you mentioned were hens! Were they to count the grains of incense? or to knock Thallus down?

48. You assert also that by promising to heal her I inveigled to my house a free woman who suffered from the same disease as Thallus; that she, too, fell senseless as a result of my incantations. It appears to me that you are accusing a wrestler not a magician, since you say that all who visited me had a fall. And yet Themison, who is a physician and who brought the woman for my inspection, denied, when you asked him, Maximus, that I had done anything to the woman other than ask her whether she heard noises in her ears, and if so, which ear suffered most. He added that she departed immediately after telling me that her right ear was most troubled in that way. At this point, Maximus, although I have for the present been careful to

abstain from praising you, lest I should seem to have flattered you with an eye to winning my case, yet I cannot help praising you for the astuteness of your questions. After they had spent much time in discussing these points and asserting that I had bewitched the woman, and after the doctor who was present on that occasion had denied that I had done so, you, with shrewdness more than human, asked them what profit I derived from my incantations. They replied, 'The woman had a fit.' 'What then?' you asked, 'Did she die?' 'No,' said they. 'What is your point then? How did the fact of her having a fit profit Apuleius?' That third question showed brilliant penetration and persistence. You knew that it was necessary to submit all facts to stringent examination of their causes, that often facts are admitted while motives remain to seek, and that the representatives of litigants are called pleaders of *causes*, because they set forth the causes of each particular act. To deny a fact is easy and needs no advocate, but it is far more arduous and difficult a task to demonstrate the rightness or wrongness of a given action. It is waste of time, therefore, to inquire whether a thing was done, when, even if it were done, no evil motive can be alleged. Under such circumstances, if no criminal motive is forthcoming, a good judge releases the accused from all further vexatious inquiry. So now, since they have not proved that I either bewitched the woman or caused her to have a fit, I for my part will not deny that I examined her at the request of a physician; and I will tell you, Maximus, why I asked her if she had noises in her ears. I will do this not so much to clear myself of the charge which you, Maximus, have already decided to involve neither blame nor guilt, as to impart to you something worthy of your hearing and interesting to one of your erudition. I will tell you in as few words as possible. I have only to call your attention to certain facts. To instruct you would be presumption.

49. The philosopher Plato, in his glorious work, the *Timaeus*, sets forth with more than mortal eloquence the constitution of the whole universe. After discoursing with great insight on the three powers that make up man's soul, and showing with the utmost clearness the divine purpose that shaped our various members, he treats of the causes of all diseases under three heads. The first cause lies in the elements of the body, when the actual qualities of those elements, moisture and cold and their two opposites, fail to harmonize. That comes to pass when one of these elements assumes undue proportions or moves from its proper place. The second cause of disease lies in the vitiation of those components of the body which, though formed out of the simple elements, have coalesced in such a manner as to have a specific character of their own, such as blood, entrails, bone, marrow, and the various substances made from the blending of each of these. Thirdly, the concretion in the body of various juices, turbid vapours, and dense humours is the last provocative of sickness.

50. Of these causes that which contributes most to epilepsy, the disease of which I set out to speak, is a condition when the flesh is so melted by the noxious influence of fire as to form a thick and foaming humour. This generates a vapour, and the heat of the air thus compressed within the body causes a white and eruptive ferment. If this ferment succeeds in escaping from the body, it is dispersed in a manner that is repulsive rather than dangerous. For it causes an eczema to break out upon the surface of the skin of the breast and mottles it with all kinds of blotches. But the person to whom this happens is never again attacked with epilepsy, and so he rids himself of a most sore disease of the spirit at the price of a slight disfigurement of the body. But if, on the other hand, this dangerous corruption[16] be contained within the body and mingle with the black bile, and so run fiercely through every vein, and then working its way upwards to the head flood the brain with its destructive stream, it straightway weakens that royal part of man's spirit which is endowed with the power of reason and is enthroned in the head of man, that is its citadel and palace. For it overwhelms and throws into confusion those channels of divinity and paths of wisdom. During sleep it makes less havoc, but when men are full of meat and wine it makes its presence somewhat unpleasantly felt by a choking sensation, the herald of epilepsy. But if it reaches such strength as to attack the heads of men when they are wide awake, then their minds grow dull with a sudden cloud of stupefaction and they fall to the ground, their bodies swooning as in death, their spirit fainting within them. Men of our race have styled it not only the 'Great sickness' and the 'Comitial sickness', but also the 'Divine sickness', in this resembling the Greeks, who call it ἱερὰ νόσος, the holy sickness. The name is just; for this sickness does outrage to the rational part of the soul, which is by far the most holy.

51. You recognize, Maximus, the theory of Plato, as far as I have been able to give it a lucid explanation in the time at my disposal. I put my trust in him when he says that the cause of epilepsy is the overflowing of this pestilential humour into the head. My inquiry therefore was, I think, reasonable when I asked the woman whether her head felt heavy, her neck numb, her temples throbbing, her ears full of noises. The fact that she acknowledged these noises to be more frequent in her right ear was proof that the disease had gone home. For the right-hand organs of the body are the strongest, and therefore their infection with the disease leaves small hope of recovery. Indeed Aristotle has left it on record in his *Problems* that whenever in the case of epileptics the disease begins on the right side, their cure is very difficult. It would be tedious were I to repeat the opinion of Theophrastus also on the subject of epilepsy. For he has left a most excellent treatise on convulsions. He asserts, however, in another book on the subject of animals ill-disposed towards mankind, that the skins of newts—which like other reptiles they shed at fixed intervals for the renewal of their youth—form a remedy for fits.

But unless you snatch up the skin as soon as it be shed, they straightway turn upon it and devour it, whether from a malign foreknowledge of its value to men or from a natural taste for it. I have mentioned these things, I have been careful to quote the arguments of renowned philosophers, and to mention the books where they are to be found, and have avoided any reference to the works of physicians or poets, that my adversaries may cease to wonder that philosophers have learnt the causes of remedies and diseases in the natural course of their researches. Well then, since this woman was brought to be examined by me in the hope that she might be cured, and since it is clear both from the evidence of the physician who brought her and from the arguments I have just set forth that such a course was perfectly right, my opponents must needs assert that it is the part of a magician and evildoer to heal disease, or, if they do not dare to say that, must confess that their accusations in regard to this epileptic boy and woman are false, absurd, and indeed epileptic.

52. Yes, Aemilianus, if you would hear the truth, *you* are the real sufferer from the falling sickness, so often have your false accusations failed and cast you helpless to the ground. Bodily collapse is no worse than intellectual, and it is as important to keep one's head as to keep one's feet, while it is as unpleasant to be loathed by this distinguished gathering as to be spat upon in one's own chamber. But you perhaps think yourself sane because you are not confined within doors, but follow the promptings of your madness whithersoever it lead you: and yet compare your frenzy with that of Thallus; you will find that there is but little to choose between you, save that Thallus confines his frenzy to himself, while you direct yours against others; Thallus distorts his eyes, you distort the truth; Thallus contracts his hands convulsively, you not less convulsively contract with your advocates; Thallus dashes himself against the pavement, you dash yourself against the judgement-seat. In a word, whatever he does, he does in his sickness erring unconsciously; but you, wretch, commit your crimes with full knowledge and with your eyes open, such is the vehemence of the disease that inspires your actions. You bring false accusations as though they were true; you charge men with doing what has never been done; though a man's innocence be clear to you as daylight, you denounce him as though he were guilty.

53. Nay, further, though I had almost forgotten to mention it, there are certain things of which you confess your ignorance, and which nevertheless you make material for accusation as though you knew all about them. You assert that I kept something mysterious wrapped up in a handkerchief among the household gods in the house of Pontianus. You confess your ignorance as to what may have been the nature or appearance of this object; you further admit that no one ever saw it, and yet you assert that it was some instrument of magic. You are not to be congratulated on this method of procedure. Your

accusation reveals no shrewdness, and has not even the merit of impudence. Do not think so for a moment. No! it shows naught save the ill-starred madness of an embittered spirit and the pitiable fury of cantankerous old age. The words you used in the presence of so grave and perspicacious a judge amounted to something very like this. 'Apuleius kept certain things wrapped in a cloth among the household gods in the house of Pontianus. Since I do not know what they were, I therefore argue that they were magical. I beg you to believe what I say, because I am talking of that of which I know nothing.' What a wonderful argument, in itself an obvious refutation of the charge. 'It must have been this, because I do not know what it was.' You are the only person hitherto discovered who knows that which he does not know. You so far surpass all others in folly, that whereas philosophers of the most keen and penetrating intellect assert that we should not trust even the objects that we see, you make statements about things which you have never seen or heard. If Pontianus still lived and you were to ask him what the cloth contained, he would reply that he did not know. There is the freedman who still has charge of the keys of the place; he is one of your witnesses, but he says that he has never examined these objects, although, as the servant responsible for the books kept there, he opened and shut the doors almost daily, continually entered the room, not seldom in my company but more often alone, and saw the cloth lying on the table unprotected by seal or cord. Quite natural, was it not? Magical objects were concealed in the cloth, and for that reason I took little care for its safe custody, but left it about anyhow for any one to examine and inspect, if he liked, or even to carry it away! I entrusted it to the custody of others, I left it to others to dispose of at their pleasure! What credence do you expect us to give you after this? Are we to believe that you, on whom I have never set eyes save in this court, know that of which Pontianus, who actually lived under the same roof, was ignorant? or shall we believe that you, who have never so much as approached the room where they were placed, have seen what the freedman never saw, although he had every opportunity to inspect them during the sedulous performance of his duties? In a word, that which you never saw must have been what you assert it to have been! And yet, you fool, if this very day you had succeeded in getting that handkerchief into your hands, I should deny the magical nature of whatever you might produce from it.

54. I give you full leave; invent what you like, rack your memory and your imagination to discover something that might conceivably seem to be of a magical nature. Even then, should you succeed in so doing, I should argue the point with you. I should say that the object in question had been substituted by you for the original, or that it had been given as a remedy, or that it was a sacred emblem that had been placed in my keeping, or that a vision had bidden me to carry it thus. There are a thousand other ways in which I might refute you with perfect truth and without giving any

explanation which is abnormal or lies outside the limits of common observation. You are now demanding that a circumstance, which, even if it were proved up to the hilt, would not prejudice me in the eyes of a good judge, should be fatal to me when, as it is, it rests on vague suspicion, uncertainty, and ignorance. You will perhaps, as is your wont, say, 'What, then, was it that you wrapped in a linen cloth and were so careful to deposit with the household gods?' Really, Aemilianus! is this the way you accuse your victims? You produce no definite evidence yourself, but ask the accused for explanations of everything. 'Why do you search for fish? Why did you examine a sick woman? What had you hidden in your handkerchief?' Did you come here to accuse me or to ask me questions? If to accuse me, prove your charges yourself; if to ask questions, do not anticipate the truth by expressing opinions on that concerning which your ignorance compels you to inquire. If this precedent be followed, if there is no necessity for the accuser to prove anything, but on the contrary he is given every facility for asking questions of the accused, there is not a man in all the world but will be indicted on some charge or other. In fact, everything that he has ever done will be used as a handle against any man who is charged with sorcery. Have you written a petition on the thigh of some statue? You are a sorcerer! Else why did you write it? Have you breathed silent prayers to heaven in some temple? You are a sorcerer! Else tell us what you asked for? Or take the contrary line. You uttered no prayer in some temple! You are a sorcerer! Else why did you not ask the gods for something? The same argument will be used if you have made some votive dedication, or offered sacrifice, or carried sprigs of some sacred plant. The day will fail me if I attempt to go through all the different circumstances of which, on these lines, the false accuser will demand an explanation. Above all, whatever object he has kept concealed or stored under lock and key at home will be asserted by the same argument to be of a magical nature, or will be dragged from its cupboard into the light of the law-court before the seat of judgement.

55. I might discourse at greater length on the nature and importance of such accusations, on the wide range for slander that this path opens for Aemilianus, on the floods of perspiration that this one poor handkerchief, contrary to its natural duty, will cause his innocent victims! But I will follow the course I have already pursued. I will acknowledge what there is no necessity for me to acknowledge, and will answer Aemilianus' questions. You ask, Aemilianus, what I had in that handkerchief. Although I might deny that I had deposited any handkerchief of mine in Pontianus' library, or even admitting that it was true enough that I did so deposit it, I might still deny that there was anything wrapped up in it. If I should take this line, you have no evidence or argument whereby to refute me, for there is no one who has ever handled it, and only one freedman, according to your own assertion, who has ever seen it. Still, as far as I am concerned I will admit the cloth to

have been full to bursting. Imagine yourself, please, to be on the brink of a great discovery, like the comrades of Ulysses who thought they had found a treasure when they stole the bag that contained all the winds. Would you like me to tell you what I had wrapped up in a handkerchief and entrusted to the care of Pontianus' household gods? You shall have your will. I have been initiated into various of the Greek mysteries, and preserve with the utmost care certain emblems and mementoes of my initiation with which the priests presented me. There is nothing abnormal or unheard of in this. Those of you here present who have been initiated into the mysteries of father Liber alone, know what you keep hidden at home, safe from all profane touch and the object of your silent veneration. But I, as I have said, moved by my religious fervour and my desire to know the truth, have learned mysteries of many a kind, rites in great number, and diverse ceremonies. This is no invention on the spur of the moment; nearly three years since, in a public discourse on the greatness of Aesculapius delivered by me during the first days of my residence at Oea, I made the same boast and recounted the number of the mysteries I knew. That discourse was thronged, has been read far and wide, is in all men's hands, and has won the affections of the pious inhabitants of Oea not so much through any eloquence of mine as because it treats of Aesculapius. Will any one, who chances to remember it, repeat the beginning of that particular passage in my discourse? You hear, Maximus, how many voices supply the words. I will order this same passage to be read aloud, since by the courteous expression of your face you show that you will not be displeased to hear it. (*The passage is read aloud.*)

56. Can any one, who has the least remembrance of the nature of religious rites, be surprised that one who has been initiated into so many holy mysteries should preserve at home certain talismans associated with these ceremonies, and should wrap them in a linen cloth, the purest of coverings for holy things? For wool, produced by the most stolid of creatures and stripped from the sheep's back, the followers of Orpheus and Pythagoras are for that very reason forbidden to wear as being unholy and unclean. But flax, the purest of all growths and among the best of all the fruits of the earth, is used by the holy priests of Egypt, not only for clothing and raiment, but as a veil for sacred things. And yet I know that some persons, among them that fellow Aemilianus, think it a good jest to mock at things divine. For I learn from certain men of Oea who know him, that to this day he has never prayed to any god or frequented any temple, while if he chances to pass any shrine, he regards it as a crime to raise his hand to his lips in token of reverence. He has never given firstfruits of crops or vines or flocks to any of the gods of the farmer, who feed him and clothe him; his farm holds no shrine, no holy place, nor grove. But why do I speak of groves or shrines? Those who have been on his property say they never saw there one stone where offering of oil has been made, one bough where wreaths have been hung. As a result,

two nicknames have been given him: he is called Charon, as I have said, on account of his truculence of spirit and of countenance, but he is also—and this is the name he prefers—called Mezentius, because he despises the gods. I therefore find it the easier to understand that he should regard my list of initiations in the light of a jest. It is even possible that, thanks to his rejection of things divine, he may be unable to induce himself to believe that it is true that I guard so reverently so many emblems and relics of mysterious rites. I care not a straw what Mezentius may think of me; but to others I make this announcement clearly and unshrinkingly. If any of you that are here present had any part with me in these same solemn ceremonies, give a sign and you shall hear what it is I keep thus. For no thought of personal safety shall induce me to reveal to the uninitiated the secrets that I have received and sworn to conceal.

57. I have, I think, Maximus, said enough to satisfy the most prejudiced of men and, as far as the handkerchief is concerned, have cleared myself of every speck of guilt. I shall run no risk in passing from the suspicions of Aemilianus to the evidence of Crassus, which my accusers read out next as if it were of the utmost importance. You heard them read from a written deposition, the evidence of a gorging brute, a hopeless glutton, named Junius Crassus, that I performed certain nocturnal rites at his house in company with my friend Appius Quintianus, who had taken lodgings there. This, mark you, Crassus says that he discovered (in spite of the fact that he was as far away as Alexandria at the time!) from finding the feathers of birds and traces of the smoke of a torch. I suppose that while he was enjoying a round of festivities at Alexandria—for Crassus is one who is ready even to encroach upon the daylight with his gluttonies—I suppose, I say, that there from his reeking tavern he espied, with eye keen as any fowler's, feathers of birds wafted towards him from his house, and saw the smoke of his home rising far off from his ancestral roof-tree. If he saw this with his eyes, he saw even further than Ulysses prayed and yearned to see. For Ulysses spent years in gazing vainly from the shore to see the smoke rising from his home, while Crassus during a few months' absence from home succeeded, without the least difficulty, in seeing this same smoke as he sat in a wine-shop! If, on the other hand, it was his nose discerned the smoke, he surpasses hounds and vultures in the keenness of his sense of smell. For what hound, what vulture hovering in the Alexandrian sky, could sniff out anything so far distant as Oea? Crassus is, I admit, a *gourmand* of the first order, and an expert in all the varied flavours of kitchen-smoke, but in view of his love of drinking, his only real title to fame, it would have been easier for the fumes of his wine, rather than the fumes of his chimney, to reach him at Alexandria.

58. Even he saw that this would pass belief. For he is said to have sold this evidence before eight in the morning while he was still fasting from food and

drink! And so he wrote that he had made his discovery in the following manner. On his return from Alexandria he went straight to his house, which Quintianus had by this time left. There in the entrance-hall he came across a large quantity of birds' feathers: the walls, moreover, were blackened with soot. He asked the reason of this from the slave whom he had left at Oea, and the latter informed him of the nocturnal rites carried out by myself and Quintianus. What an ingenious lie! What a probable invention! That I, had I wished to do anything of the sort, should have done it there rather than in my own house! That Quintianus, who is supporting me here to-day, and whom I mention with the greatest respect and honour for the close love that binds him to me, for his deep erudition and consummate eloquence, that this same Quintianus, supposing him to have dined off some birds or, as they assert, killed them for magical purposes, should have had no slave to sweep up the feathers and throw them out of doors! Or further that the smoke should have been strong enough to blacken the walls and that Quintianus should have suffered such defacement of the room in which he slept, while it was still in his occupation! Nonsense, Aemilianus! There is no probability in the story, unless indeed Crassus on his return went not to the bedroom, but after his fashion made straight for the kitchen. And what made his slave suspect that the walls had been blackened by night in particular? Was it the colour of the smoke? Does night smoke differ from day smoke in being darker? And why did so suspicious and conscientious a slave allow Quintianus to leave the house before having it cleaned? Why did those feathers lie like lead and await the arrival of Crassus for so long? Let not Crassus accuse his slave. It is much more likely that he himself fabricated this mendacious nonsense about feathers and soot, being unable even in his evidence to divorce himself further from his kitchen.

59. And why did you read out this evidence from a written deposition? Where in the world is Crassus? Has he returned to Alexandria out of disgust at the state of his house? Is he washing his walls? or, as is more likely, is the glutton feeling ill after his debauch? I myself saw him yesterday here at Sabrata hiccoughing in your face, Aemilianus, in the most conspicuous manner in the middle of the market-place. Pray, Maximus, ask your slaves whose duty it is to keep you informed of people's names—although, I admit, Crassus is better known to the keepers of taverns—yet ask them, I say, whether they have ever seen Junius Crassus, a citizen of Oea, in this place. They will answer 'yes'. Let Aemilianus then produce this most admirable young man on whose testimony he relies. You notice the time of day. I tell you that Crassus has long since been snoring in a drunken slumber or has taken a second bathe and is now evaporating the sweat of intoxication at the bath that he may be equal to a fresh drinking bout after supper. He presents himself in writing only. That is the way he speaks to you, Maximus. Even he is not so dead to sense of shame as to be able to lie to your face without a

blush. But there is perhaps another reason for his absence. He may have been unable to abstain from the wine-cup[17] sufficiently long to keep sober against this moment; or it may be that Aemilianus took good care not to subject him to your severe and searching gaze, lest you should damn the brute with his close-shaven cheeks and his disgusting appearance by a mere glance at his face, when you saw a young man with his features stripped of the beard and hair that should adorn them, his eyes heavy with wine, his lids swollen, his broad[18] grin, his slobbering lips, his harsh voice, his trembling hands, his breath[19] reeking of the cook-shop. He has long since devoured his fortune; nothing is left him of his patrimony save a house that serves him for the sale of his false witness, and never did he make a more remunerative contract than he has done with regard to this evidence he offers to-day. For he sold Aemilianus his drunken fictions for 3,000 sesterces, as every one at Oea is aware.

60. We all knew of this before it actually took place. I might have prevented the transaction by denouncing it, but I knew that so foolish a lie would be prejudicial to Aemilianus, who wasted his money to secure it, rather than to myself, who treated it with the contempt it deserved. I wished not only that Aemilianus should lose his money, but that Crassus should have his reputation ruined by his disgraceful perjury. It was but the day before yesterday that the transaction took place in the most open manner at the house of Rufinus, of whom I shall soon have something to say. Rufinus and Calpurnianus acted as middlemen and arranged the bargain.[20] The former carried out the task with all the more readiness because he was certain that his wife, at whose misconduct he knowingly connives, would be sure to recover from Crassus a large proportion of his fee for perjury. I noticed that you also, Maximus, suspected with your usual acuteness that they, as soon as this written evidence was produced, had formed a league and conspiracy against me; and I saw from your face that the whole affair excited your disgust. Finally my accusers, in spite of their being paragons of audacity and monsters of shamelessness, did not dare to read out Crassus' evidence in full or to build anything upon it; for they saw that at the mention of his name you smelt a rat. I have mentioned these facts not because I am afraid of these dreadful feathers and stains of soot—least of all with you to judge me—but that Crassus might meet with due punishment for having sold mere smoke to a helpless rustic like Aemilianus.

61. Their next[21] charge concerns the manufacture of a seal which they produced when they read Pudentilla's letters. This seal, they assert, I had fashioned of the rarest wood by some secret process for purposes of the black art. They add that, although it is loathly and horrible to look upon, being in the form of a skeleton, I yet give it especial honour and call it in the Greek tongue, βασιλεύς, my king. I think I am right in saying that I am

following the various stages of their accusation in due order and reconstructing the whole fabric of their slander detail by detail.

Now how can the manufacture of this seal have been secret, as you assert, when you are sufficiently well acquainted with the maker to have summoned him to appear in court? Here is Cornelius Saturninus, the artist, a man whose skill is famous among his townsfolk and whose character is above reproach. A little while back, in answer, Maximus, to your careful cross-examination, he explained the whole sequence of events in the most convincing and truthful manner. He said that I visited his shop and, after looking at many geometrical patterns all carved out of boxwood in the most cunning and ingenious manner, was so much attracted by his skill that I asked him to make me certain mechanical devices and also begged him to make me the image of some god to which I might pray after my custom. The particular god and the precise material I left to his choice, my only stipulation being that it should be made of wood. He therefore first attempted to work in boxwood. Meanwhile, during my absence in the country, Sicinius Pontianus, my step-son, wishing to gratify me,[22] procured some ebony tablets from that excellent lady Capitolina and brought them to his shop, exhorting him to make what I had ordered out of this rarer and more durable material: such a gift, he said, would be most gratifying to me. Our artist did as Pontianus suggested, as far as the size of the ebony tablets permitted. By careful dove-tailing of minute portions of the tablets he succeeded in making a small figure of Mercury.

62. You heard all the evidence just as I repeat it. Moreover it receives exact confirmation from the answers given to you in cross-examination by Capitolina's son, a youth of the most excellent character, who is here in court to-day. He said that Pontianus asked for the tablets, that Pontianus took them to the artist Saturninus. Nor does he deny that Pontianus received the completed signet from Saturninus and afterwards gave it me. All these things have been openly and manifestly proved. What remains, in which any suspicion of sorcery can lie concealed? Nay, what is there that does not absolutely convict you of obvious falsehood? You said that the seal was of secret manufacture, whereas Pontianus, a distinguished member of the equestrian order, gave the commission for it. The figure was carved in public by Saturninus as he sat in his shop. He is a man of sterling character and recognized honesty. The work was assisted by the munificence of a distinguished married lady, and many both among the slaves and the acquaintances who frequented my house were aware both of the commission for the work and its execution. You were not ashamed falsely to pretend that I had searched high and low for the requisite wood through all the town, although you know that I was absent from Oea at that time, and although it has been proved that I gave a free hand as to the material.

63. Your third lie was that the figure which was made was the lean, eviscerated frame of a gruesome corpse, utterly horrible and ghastly as any goblin. If you had discovered such definite proof of my sorceries, why did you not insist on my producing it in court? Was it that you might have complete freedom for inventing lies in the absence of the subject of your slanders? If so, the opportunity afforded you for mendacity has been lost you, thanks to a certain habit of mine which comes in most opportunely. It is my wont wherever I go to carry with me the image of some god hidden among my books and to pray to him on feast days with offerings of incense and wine and sometimes even of victims. When, therefore, I heard persistent though outrageously mendacious assertions that the figure I carried was that of a skeleton, I ordered some one to go and bring from my house my little image of Mercury, the same that Saturninus had made for me at Oea. You there, give it them! Let them see it, hold it, examine it. There you see the image which that scoundrel called a skeleton. Do you hear these cries of protest that arise from all present? Do you hear the condemnation of your lie? Are you not at last ashamed of all your slanders? Is this a skeleton, this a goblin, is this the familiar spirit you asserted it to be? Is this a magic symbol or one that is common and ordinary? Take it, I beg you, Maximus, and examine it. It is good that a holy thing should be entrusted to hands as pure and pious as yours. See there, how fair it is to view, how full of all a wrestler's grace and vigour! How cheerful is the god's face, how comely the down that creeps on either side his cheeks, how the curled hair shows upon his head beneath the shadow of his hat's brim, how neatly the tiny pair of pinions project about his brows, how daintily the cloak is drawn about his shoulders! He who dares call this a skeleton, either never sees an image of a god or if he does ignores it. Indeed, he who thinks this to represent a goblin must have goblins on the brain.

64. But in return for that lie, Aemilianus, may that same god who goes between the lords of heaven and the lords of hell grant you the hatred of the gods of either world and ever send to meet you the shadows of the dead with all the ghosts, with all the fiends, with all the spectres, with all the goblins of all the world, and thrust upon your eyes all the terror that walketh by night, all the dread dwellers in the tomb, all the horrors of the sepulchre, although your age and character have brought you near enough to them already. But we of the family of Plato know naught save what is bright and joyous, majestic and heavenly and of the world above us. Nay, in its zeal to reach the heights of wisdom, the Platonic school has explored regions higher than heaven itself and has stood triumphant on the outer circumference of this our universe. Maximus knows that I speak truth, for in his careful study of the *Phaedrus* he has read of the 'place that is higher than heaven, being builded on heaven's back.' Maximus also clearly understands—I am now going to reply to your accusation about the name—who he is whom not I but Plato

was first to call the 'King'. 'All things,' he says, 'depend upon the King of all things and for him only all things exist.' Maximus knows who that 'King' is, even the cause and reason and primal origin of all nature, the lord and father of the soul, the eternal saviour of all that lives, the unwearying builder of his world. Yet builds he without labour, yet saves he without care, he is father without begetting, he knows no limitation of space or time or change, and therefore few may conceive and none may tell of his power.

65. I will even go out of my way to aggravate the suspicion of sorcery; I will not tell you, Aemilianus, who it is that I worship as my king. Even if the proconsul should ask me himself who my god is, I am dumb.

About the name I have said enough for the present. For the rest I know that some of my audience are anxious to hear why I wanted the figure made not of silver or gold, but only of wood, though I think that their desire springs not so much from their anxiety to see me cleared of guilt as from eagerness for knowledge. They would like to have this last doubt removed, even although they see that I have amply rebutted all suspicion of any crime. Listen, then, you who would know, but listen with all the sharpness and attention that you may, for you are to hear the very words that Plato wrote in his old age in the last book of the *Laws*. 'The man of moderate means when he makes offerings to the gods should do so in proportion to his means. Now, earth and the household hearths of all men are holy to all the gods. Let no one therefore dedicate any shrines to the gods over and above these.' He forbids this with the purpose of preventing men from venturing to build private shrines; for he thinks that the public temples suffice his citizens for the purposes of sacrifice. He then continues, 'Gold and silver in other cities, whether in the keeping of private persons or of temples, are invidious possessions; ivory taken from a body wherefrom the life has passed is not a welcome offering; iron and bronze are instruments of war. Whatsoever a man dedicates, let it be of wood and wood only, or if it be of stone, of stone only.' The general murmur of assent shows, O Maximus, and you, gentlemen, who have the honour to assist him, that I am adjudged to have made admirable use of Plato, not only as a guide in life, but as an advocate in court, to whose instructions, as you see, I give implicit obedience.

66. It is now time for me to turn first and foremost to the letters of Pudentilla, or rather to retrace the whole course of events a little further back still. For I desire to make it abundantly clear that I, whom they keep accusing of having forced my way into Pudentilla's house solely through love of money, ought really never to have come near that house, had the thought of money ever crossed my mind. My marriage has for many reasons brought me the reverse of prosperity and, but for the fact that my wife's virtues are compensation for any number of disadvantages, might be described as disastrous.

Disappointment and envy are the sole causes that have involved me in this trial, and even before that gathered many mortal perils about my path. What motives for resentment has Aemilianus against me, even assuming him to be correctly informed when he accuses me of magic? No least word of mine has ever injured him in such a way as to give him the appearance of pursuing a just revenge. It is certainly no lofty ambition that prompts him to accuse me, ambition such as fired Marcus Antonius to accuse Cnaeus Carbo, Caius Mucius to accuse Aulus Albucius, Publius Sulpicius to accuse Cnaeus Norbanus, Caius Furius to accuse Manius Aquilius, Caius Curio to accuse Quintus Metellus. They were young men of admirable education and were led by ambition to undertake these accusations as the first step in a forensic career, that by the conduct of some *cause célèbre* they might make themselves a name among their fellow citizens. This privilege was conceded by antiquity to young men just entering public life as a means of winning glory for their youthful genius. The custom has long since become obsolete, but even if the practice were still common, it would not apply to Aemilianus. It would not have been becoming to him to make any display of his eloquence, for he is rude and unlettered; nor to show a passion for renown, since he is a mere barbarian bumpkin; nor thus to open his career as an advocate, for he is an old man on the brink of the grave. The only hypothesis creditable to him would be that he is perhaps giving an example of his austerity of character and has undertaken this accusation through sheer hatred of wrongdoing and to assert his own integrity. But I should hardly accept such an hypothesis even in the case of a greater Aemilianus, not our African friend here, but the conqueror of Africa and Numantia, who held, moreover, the office of censor at Rome. Much less will I believe that this dull blockhead, I will not say, hates sin, but recognizes it when he sees it.

67. What then was his motive? It is as clear as day to any one that envy is the sole motive that has spurred him and Herennius Rufinus, his instigator—of whom I shall have more to say later—and the rest of my enemies, to fabricate these false charges of sorcery.

Well, there are five points which I must discuss. If I remember aright, their accusations as regards Pudentilla were as follows. Firstly, they said that after the death of her first husband she resolutely set her face against re-marriage, but was seduced by my incantations. Secondly, there are her letters, which they regard as an admission that I used sorcery. Thirdly and fourthly, they object that she made a love-match at the advanced age of sixty and that the marriage contract was sealed not in the town but at a country house. Lastly, there is the most invidious of all these accusations, namely, that which concerns the dowry. It is into this charge they have put all their force and all their venom; it is this that vexes them most of all. They assert that at the very outset of our wedded life I forced my devoted wife in the absolute seclusion of her country house to make over to me a large dowry. I will show that all these statements are so false, so worthless, so unsubstantial, and I shall refute them so easily and unquestionably, that in good truth, Maximus, and you, gentlemen, his assessors, I fear you may think that I have suborned my accusers to bring these charges, that I might have the opportunity of publicly dispelling the hatred of which I am the victim. I will ask you to believe *now*, what you will understand when the facts are before you, that I shall need to put out all my strength to prevent you from thinking that such a baseless accusation is a cunning device of my own rather than a stupid enterprise of my enemies.

68. I shall now briefly retrace events and force Aemilianus himself to admit, when he has heard the facts, that his envy was groundless and that he has strayed far from the truth. In the meantime I beg you, as you have already done, or if possible yet more than you have already done, to give the best of your attention to me as I trace the whole case to its fount and source.

Aemilia Pudentilla, now my wife, was once the wife of a certain Sicinius Amicus. By him she had two sons, Pontianus and Pudens. These two boys were left by their father's death under the guardianship of their paternal grandfather—for Amicus predeceased his father—and were brought up by their mother with remarkable care and affection for about fourteen years. She was in the flower of her age, and it was not of her own choosing that she remained a widow for so long. But the boys' grandfather was eager that she should, in spite of her reluctance, take his son, Sicinius Clarus, for her second husband[23] and with this in view kept all other suitors at a distance. He further threatened her that if she married elsewhere he would by his will exclude her sons from the possession of any of their father's heritage. When she saw that nothing could move him to alter the condition that he had laid down, such was her wisdom, and so admirable her maternal affection, that to prevent her sons' interests suffering any damage in this respect, she made a contract of marriage with Sicinius Clarus in accordance with her father-in-law's bidding, but by various evasions managed to avoid the marriage until the boys' grandfather died, leaving them as his heirs, with the result that Pontianus, the elder son, became his brother's guardian.

69. She was now freed from all embarrassment, and being sought in marriage by many distinguished persons resolved to remain a widow no longer. The dreariness of her solitary life she might have borne, but her bodily infirmities had become intolerable. This chaste and saintly lady, after so many years of blameless widowhood, without even a breath of scandal, owing to her long absence from a husband's embraces, began to suffer internal pains so severe that they brought her to the brink of the grave. Doctors and wise women agreed that the disease had its origin in her long widowhood, that the evil was increasing daily and her sickness steadily assuming a more serious

character; the remedy was that she should marry before her youth finally departed from her. There were many who welcomed this recommendation, but none more so than that fellow Aemilianus, who a little while back asserted with the most unhesitating mendacity that Pudentilla had never thought of marriage until I compelled her to be mine by my exercise of the black art; that I alone had been found to outrage the virgin purity of her widowhood by incantations and love philtres. I have often heard it said with truth that a liar should have a good memory. Had you forgotten, Aemilianus, that before I came to Oea, you wrote to her son Pontianus, who had then attained to man's estate and was pursuing his studies at Rome, suggesting that she should marry? Give me the letter, or better give it to Aemilianus and let him refute himself in his own voice with his own words.

Is this your letter? Why do you turn pale? We know you are past blushing. Is this your signature? Read a little louder, please, that all may realize how his written words belie his speech and how much more he is at variance with himself than with me.

70. Did you, Aemilianus, write what has just been read out? 'I know that she is willing to marry and that she ought to do so, but I do not know the object of her choice.' You were right there. You knew nothing about it. For Pudentilla, though she admitted that she wished to marry again, said nothing to you about her suitor. She knew the intrusive malignity of your nature too well. But you still expected her to marry your brother Clarus and were induced by your false hopes to go further and to urge her son to assent to the match. And of course, if she had wedded Clarus, a boorish and decrepit old man, you would have asserted that she had long desired to marry him of her own free will without the intervention of any magic. But now that she has married a young man of the elegance which you attribute to him, you say that she had always refused to marry and must have done so under compulsion! You did not know, you villain, that the letter you had written on the subject was being preserved, you did not know that you would be convicted by your own testimony. The fact is that Pudentilla, knowing your changeableness and unreliability no less than your shamelessness and mendacity, rather than forward the letter preferred to keep it as clear evidence of your intentions, and wrote a letter of her own on the same subject to her son Pontianus at Rome, in which she gave full reasons for her determination. She told him pretty fully about the state of her health; there was no longer any reason for her to persist in remaining a widow; she had so remained for thus long and had sacrificed her health solely to procure him the inheritance of his grandfather's fortune, a fortune to which she had by the exercise of the greatest care made considerable additions: Pontianus himself was now by the grace of heaven ripe for marriage and his brother for the garb of manhood. She begged them to suffer her at length to solace her

lonely existence and to relieve her ill health: they need have no fears as to her final choice or as to her motherly affection; she would still be as a wife what she had been as a widow. I will order a copy of this letter to her son to be read aloud. (*The letter is read.*)

71. This letter makes it, I think, sufficiently clear that it needed no incantations of mine to move Pudentilla from her resolve to remain a widow, but that she had been for some time by no means averse to marriage, when she chose me—it may be in preference to others. I cannot see why such a choice by so excellent a woman should be brought against me as matter for reproach rather than honour. But I admit feeling surprise that Aemilianus and Rufinus should be annoyed at the lady's decision, when those who were actually suitors for her hand acquiesce in her preference for myself. She was indeed guided in making her choice less by her personal inclination than by the advice of her son, a fact which Aemilianus cannot deny. For Pontianus on receiving his mother's letter hastily flew hither from Rome, fearing that, if the man of her choice proved to be avaricious, she might, as often happens, transfer her whole fortune to the house of her new husband. This anxiety tormented him not a little. All his own expectations of wealth together with those of his brother depended on his mother. His grandfather had left but a moderate fortune, his mother possessed 4,000,000 sesterces. Of this sum, it is true, she owed a considerable portion to her sons, but they had no security for this, relying—naturally enough—on her word alone. He gave but silent expression to his fears; he did not venture to show any open opposition for fear of seeming to distrust her.

72. Things being in this delicate position owing to the matrimonial intentions of the mother and the fears of the son, chance or destiny brought me to Oea on my way to Alexandria. Did not my respect for my wife prevent me, I would say 'Would God it had never happened'. It was winter when this occurred. Overcome by the fatigues of the journey, I was laid up for a considerable number of days in the house of my friends the Appii, whom I name to show the affection and esteem with which I regard them. There Pontianus came to see me; for not so very long before certain common friends had introduced him to me at Athens, and we had afterwards lodged together and come to know each other intimately. He greeted me with the utmost courtesy, inquired anxiously after my health, and touched dexterously on the subject of love. For he thought that he had found an ideal husband for his mother to whom he could without the slightest risk entrust the whole fortune of the house. At first he sounded me as to my inclinations in somewhat ambiguous language, and seeing that I was desirous of resuming my journey and was not in the least disposed to take a wife, he begged me at any rate to remain at Oea for a little while, as he himself was desirous of travelling with me. Since my physical infirmity had made it impossible for

me to profit by the present winter, he urged that it would be well to wait for the next owing to the danger presented by the passage of the Syrtes and the risk of encountering wild beasts. His urgent entreaty induced my friends the Appii to allow me to leave them and to become his guest in his mother's house. I should find the situation healthier, he said, and should get a freer view of the sea—a special attraction in my eyes.

73. He had shown the greatest eagerness in inducing me to come to this decision, and strongly recommended his mother and his brother—that boy there—to my consideration. I gave them some help in our common studies and a marked intimacy sprang up between us. Meanwhile I gradually recovered my health. At the instance of my friends I gave a discourse in public. This took place in the basilica, which was thronged by a vast audience. I was greeted with many expressions of approval, the audience shouted 'bravo! bravo!' like one man, and besought me to remain and become a citizen of Oea. On the dispersal of the audience Pontianus approached me, and by way of prelude said that such universal enthusiasm was nothing less than a sign from heaven. He then revealed to me that it was his cherished design—with my permission—to bring about a match between myself and his mother, for whose hand there were many suitors. He added that I was the only friend in the world in whom he could put implicit trust and confidence. If I were to refuse to undertake such a responsibility, simply because it was no fair heiress that was offered me, but a woman of plain appearance and the mother of children—if I were moved by these considerations and insisted on reserving myself for a more attractive and wealthier match, my behaviour would be unworthy of a friend and a philosopher. It would take too long—even if I were willing—to tell you what I replied and how long and how frequently we conversed on the subject, with how many pressing entreaties he plied me, never ceasing until he finally won my consent. I had had ample opportunity for observing Pudentilla's character, for I had lived for a whole year continually in her company and had realized how rich was her endowment of good qualities; but my desire for travel led me to desire to refuse the match as an impediment. But I soon began to love her for her virtues as ardently as though I had wooed her of my own initiative. Pontianus had also persuaded his mother to give me the preference over all her other suitors, and showed extraordinary eagerness for the marriage to take place at the earliest possible date. We could scarcely induce him to consent to the very briefest postponement to such time as he himself should have taken a wife and his brother in due course have assumed the garb of manhood. That done, we would be married at once.

74. Would to heaven it were possible without serious damage to my case to pass by what I have now to relate. I freely forgave Pontianus when he begged for pardon, and I have no wish to seem to reproach him now for the

fickleness of his conduct. I acknowledge the truth of a circumstance brought against me by my accusers, I admit that Pontianus, after taking to himself a wife, broke his pledged word and suddenly changed his mind; that he tried to prevent the fulfilment of this project with no less obstinacy than he had shown zeal in forwarding it. He was ready to make any sacrifice, to go any lengths, to prevent our marriage taking place. Nevertheless this discreditable change of attitude, this deliberate quarrel with his mother, must not be laid to his charge, but to that of his father-in-law, Herennius Rufinus, whom you see before you, a man than whom no more worthless, wicked, and grime-stained soul lives upon this earth. I will—since I cannot avoid it—give a brief description of this man's character, using such moderation as I may, lest, if I pass him by in silence, the energy which he has shown in engineering this accusation against me should have been spent all in vain.

This is the man who poisoned that worthless boy against me, who is the prime mover in this accusation, who has hired advocates and bought witnesses. This is the furnace in which all this calumny has been forged, this the firebrand, this the scourge that has driven Aemilianus here to his task. He makes it his boast before all men in the most extravagant language that it is through his machinations that my indictment has been procured. In truth he has some reason for self-congratulation. For he is the organizer of every lawsuit, the deviser of every perjury, the architect of every lie, the seed-ground of every wickedness, the vile haunt and hideous habitation of lust and gluttony, the mark of every scandal since his earliest years: in boyhood, ere he became so hideously bald, the ready servant of the vilest vices; in youth a stage dancer limp and nerveless enough in all conscience, but, they tell me, clumsy and inartistic in his very effeminacy. Except for his immodesty he is said not to have possessed a single quality that should distinguish an actor.

75. He is older now—God's curse upon him! I crave your pardon for my warmth of language. But his house is the dwelling-place of panders, his whole household foul with sin, himself a man of infamous character, his wife a harlot, his sons like their parents. His door night and day is battered with the kicks of wanton gallants, his windows loud with the sound of loose serenades, his dining-room wild with revel, his bedchambers the haunt of adulterers. For no one need fear to enter it save he who has no gift for the husband. Thus does he make an income from his own dishonour. What else should the wretch do? He has lost a considerable fortune, though I admit that he only got that fortune unexpectedly through a fraudulent transaction on the part of his father. The latter, having borrowed money from a number of persons, preferred to keep their money at the cost of his own good name. Bills poured in on every side with demands for payment. Every one that met him laid hands on him as though he were a madman. 'Steady, now!' says he, 'I can't find the cash.' So he resigned his golden rings and all the badges of

his position in society and thus came to terms with his creditors. But he had by a most ingenious fraud transferred the greater part of his property to his wife, and so, although he himself was needy, ill-clad and protected by the very depth of his fall, managed to leave this same Rufinus—I am telling you the truth and nothing but the truth—no less than 3,000,000 sesterces to be squandered on riotous living. This was the sum that came to him unencumbered from his mother's property, over and above the daily dowry brought him by his wife. Yet all this money has been ravenously devoured by this glutton in a few short years, all this fortune has been destroyed by the infinite variety of his gormandizing; so that you might really think him to be afraid of seeming in any way to be the gainer by his father's dishonesty. This honourable fellow actually took care that what had been ill-gained should be ill-spent, nor was anything left him from his too ample fortune, save his depraved ambition and his boundless appetite.

76. His wife, however, was getting old and worn out and refused to continue to support the whole household by her own dishonour. But there was a daughter who, at her mother's instigation, was exhibited to all the wealthy young men, but in vain. Had she not come across so easy a victim as Pontianus she would perhaps still have been sitting at home a widow who had never been a bride. Pontianus, in spite of urgent attempts on our part to dissuade him, gave her the right—false and illusory though it was—to be called a bride. He did this knowing that, but a short time before he married her, she had been seduced and deserted by a young man of good family to whom she had been previously betrothed. And so his new bride came to him, not as other brides come, but unabashed and undismayed, her virtue lost, her modesty gone, her bridal-veil a mockery. Cast off by her previous lover, she brought to her wedding the name without the purity of a maid. She rode in a litter carried by eight slaves. You who were present saw how impudently she made eyes at all the young and how immodestly she flaunted her charms. Who did not recognize her mother's pupil, when they saw her dyed lips, her rouged cheeks, and her lascivious eyes? Her dowry was borrowed, every farthing of it, on the eve of her wedding, and was indeed greater than could be expected of so large and impoverished a family.

77. But though Rufinus' fortune is small, his hopes are boundless. With avarice rivalled only by his need he had already devoured Pudentilla's 4,000,000 in vain anticipation. With this in view he decided that I must be got out of the way, in order that he might find fewer obstacles in his attempt to hoodwink the weak Pontianus and the lonely Pudentilla. He began, therefore, to upbraid his son-in-law for having betrothed his mother to me. He urged him to draw back without delay from so perilous a path, while there was yet time; to keep his mother's fortune himself rather than deliberately transfer it to the keeping of a stranger. He threatened that, if he

refused, he would take away his daughter, the device of an old hand to influence a young man in love. To be brief, he so wrought upon the simple-minded young man, who was, moreover, a slave to the charms of his new bride, as to mould him to his will and move him from his purpose. Pontianus went to his mother and told her what Rufinus had said to him. But he made no impression on her steadfast character. On the contrary, she rebuked him for his fickleness and inconstancy, and it was no pleasant news he took back to his father-in-law. His mother had shown a firmness of purpose not to be expected of one of her placid disposition, and to make matters worse his expostulations had made her angry, which was likely seriously to increase her obstinacy: in fact, she had finally replied, that it was no secret to her that his expostulations were instigated by Rufinus, a fact which made the support and assistance of a husband against his desperate greed all the more necessary to her.

78. When he heard this, the ruffian was stung to fury and burst into such wild and ungovernable rage that in the presence of her own son he heaped insults, such as he might have used to his own wife, on the purest and most modest of women. In the presence of many witnesses, whom, if you desire it, I will name, he loudly denounced her as a wanton and myself as a sorcerer and poisoner, threatening to murder me with his own hands. I can hardly restrain my anger, such fierce indignation fills my soul. That you, the most effeminate of men, should threaten any man with death at your hand! Your hand! What hand! The hand of Philomela or Medea or Clytemnestra? Why, when you dance in those characters you show such contemptible timidity, you are so frightened at the sight of steel, that you will not even carry a property sword? But I am digressing. Pudentilla, seeing to her astonishment that her son had fallen lower than she could have deemed possible, went into the country and by way of rebuke wrote him the notorious letter, in which, according to my accusers, she confessed that my magical practices had made her lose her reason and fall in love with me. And yet, Maximus, the day before yesterday at your command I took a copy of the letter in the presence of witnesses and of Pontianus' secretary. Aemilianus also was there and countersigned the copy. What is the result? In contradiction to my accusers' assertion everything is found to tell in my favour.

79. And yet, even if she had spoken somewhat strongly and had called me a magician, it would be a reasonable explanation that she had, in defending her conduct to her son, preferred to allege compulsion on my part rather than her own inclination. Is Phaedra the only woman whom love has driven to write a lying letter? Is it not rather a device common to all women that, when they have begun to feel strong desire for anything of this kind, they should prefer to make themselves out the victims of compulsion? But even supposing she had genuinely regarded me as a magician, would the mere fact

of Pudentilla's writing to that effect be a reason for actually regarding me as a magician? You, with all your arguments and your witnesses and your diffuse eloquence, have failed to prove me a magician. Could she prove it with one word? A formal indictment, written and signed before a judge, is a far more weighty document than what is written in a private letter! Why do not you prove me a magician by my own deeds instead of having recourse to the mere words of another? If your principle be followed, and whatever any one may have written in a letter under the influence of love or hatred be admitted as proof, many a man will be indicted on the wildest charges. 'Pudentilla called you a magician in her letter; therefore you are a magician!' If she had called me a consul, would that make me one? What if she had called me a painter, a doctor, or even an innocent man? Would you accept any of these statements, simply because she had made them? You would accept none of them. Yet it is a gross injustice to believe a person when he speaks evil of another and to refuse to believe him when he speaks well. It is a gross injustice that a letter should have power to destroy and not to save. 'But,' says my accuser, 'she was out of her wits, she loved you distractedly.' I will grant it for the moment. But are all persons, who are the objects of love, magicians, just because the person in love with them chances to say so in a letter? If, indeed, Pudentilla wrote in a letter to another person what would clearly be prejudicial to myself, I think she could hardly have been in love with me at the moment in question.

80. Tell me now, what is your contention? Was she mad or sane when she wrote? Sane, do you say? Then she was not the victim of magic. Insane? In that case she did not know what she was writing and must not be believed. Nay, even supposing her to have been insane, she would not have been aware of the fact. For just as to say 'I am silent' is to make a fool of oneself, since these very words actually break silence, and the act of speaking impugns the substance of one's speech, so it is even more absurd to say 'I am mad'. It cannot be true unless the speaker knows what he says, and he who knows what madness is, is *ipso facto* sane. For madness cannot know itself any more than blindness can see itself. Therefore Pudentilla was in possession of her senses, if she thought she was out of them. I could say more on this point, but enough of dialectic! I will read out the letter which gives crying witness to a very different state of things and might indeed have been specially prepared to suit this particular trial. Take it and read it out until I interrupt. (*The letter is read.*)

Stop a moment before you go on to what follows. We have come to the crucial point. So far, Maximus, as far at any rate as I have noticed, the lady has made no mention of magic, but has merely repeated in the same order the statements which I quoted a short time ago about her long widowhood, the proposed remedy for her ill health, her desire to marry, the good report she had heard of me from Pontianus, his own advice that she should marry me in preference to others.

81. So much for what has been read. There remains a portion of the letter which, although like the first part it was written in my defence, also turns against me. For although it was specially written to rebut the charge of magic brought against me, a remarkable piece of ingenuity on the part of Rufinus has altered its meaning and brought me into discredit with certain citizens of Oea as being a proved sorcerer. Maximus, you have heard much from the lips of others, you have learned yet more by reading, and your own personal experience has taught you not a little. But you will say that never yet have you come across such insidious cunning or such marvellous dexterity in crime. What [Palamedes](), what [Sisyphus](), what [Eurybates]() or [Phrynondas]() could ever have devised such guile? All those whom I have mentioned, together with all the notorious deceivers of history, would seem mere [clowns and pantaloons](), were they to attempt to match this one single instance of Rufinus' craftiness. O miracle of lies! O subtlety worthy of the prison and the stocks! Who could imagine that what was written as a defence could without the alteration of a single letter be transformed into an accusation! Good God! it is incredible. But I will make clear to you how the incredible came to pass.

82. The mother was rebuking her son because, after extolling me to her as a model of all the virtues, he now, at Rufinus' instigation, asserted that I was a magician. The actual words were as follows: 'Apuleius is a magician and has bewitched me to love him. Come to me, then, while I am still in my senses!' These words, which I have quoted in Greek, have been selected by Rufinus and separated from their context. He has taken them round as a confession on the part of Pudentilla, and, with Pontianus at his side all dissolved in tears, has shown them through all the market-place, allowing men only to read that portion which I have just cited and suppressing all that comes before and after. His excuse was that the rest of the letter was too disgusting to be shown; it was sufficient that publicity should be given to Pudentilla's confession as to my sorcery. What was the result? Every one thought it probable enough. That very letter, which was written to clear my character, excited the most violent hatred against me amongst those who did not know the facts. This foul villain went rushing about in the midst of the market-place like any bacchanal; he kept opening the letter and proclaiming, 'Apuleius is a sorcerer! She herself describes her feelings and her sufferings! What more do you demand?' There was no one to take my part and reply, 'Give us the whole letter, please! Let me see it all, let me read it from beginning to end. There are many things which, produced apart from their context, may seem open to a slanderous interpretation. Any speech may be attacked, if a passage depending for its sense on what has preceded be robbed

of its commencement, or if phrases be expunged at will from the place they logically occupy, or if what is written ironically be read out in such a tone as to make it seem a defamatory statement.' With what justice this protest or words to that effect might have been uttered the actual order of the letter will show.

33. Now, Aemilianus, try to remember whether the following were not the words of which, together with myself, you took a copy in the presence of witnesses, 'For since I desired to marry for the reasons of which I told you, you persuaded me to choose Apuleius in preference to all others, since you had a great admiration for him and were eager through me to become yet more intimate with him. But now that certain ill-natured persons have brought accusations against us and attempt to dissuade you, Apuleius has suddenly become a magician and has bewitched me to love him. Come to me, then, while I am still in my senses.'

I ask you, Maximus, if letters—some of which are actually called vocal[24]—could find a voice, if words, as poets say, could take them wings and fly, would they not, when Rufinus first made disingenuous excerpts from that letter, read but a few lines and deliberately said nothing of much that bore a more favourable meaning, would not the remaining letters have cried out that they were unjustly kept out of sight? Would not the words suppressed by Rufinus have flown from his hands and filled the whole market-place with tumult, crying that they too had been sent by Pudentilla, they too had been entrusted with something to say, and calling upon men to listen to *them* instead of giving ear to a dishonest villain who was attempting to prove a lie by means of another's letter? for Pudentilla had never accused Apuleius of magic, while Rufinus' accusation was tantamount to an acquittal. All these things were not said then, but now, when they are of more effectual service to me, their truth appears clearer than day. Rufinus, your cunning stands revealed, your fraud stares us in the face, your lies are laid bare; truth dethroned for a while rises once more and slander sinks[25] downward to the bottomless pit.

34. You challenged me with Pudentilla's letter: with that letter I win the day. If you like to hear the conclusion, I will not grudge it you. Tell me, what were the words with which she ended the letter, that poor bewitched, lunatic, insane, infatuated lady? 'I am not bewitched, I am not in love; it is my destiny.'[26] Would you have anything more? Pudentilla throws your words in your teeth and publicly vindicates her sanity against your slanderous aspersions. The motive or necessity of her marriage, whichever it was, she now ascribes to fate, and between fate and magic there is a great gulf, indeed they have absolutely nothing in common. For if it be true that the destiny of each created thing is like a fierce torrent that may neither be stayed nor diverted, what power is left for magic drugs or incantations? Pudentilla,

therefore, not only denied that I was a magician, but denied the very existence of magic. It is a good thing that Pontianus, following his usual custom, kept his mother's letter safe in its entirety: it is a good thing that the speed with which this case has been hurried on left you no opportunity for adding to that letter at your leisure. For this I have to thank you and your foresight, Maximus. You saw through their slanders from the beginning and hurried on the case that they might not gather strength as the days went by; you gave them no breathing space and wrecked their designs. Suppose now that the mother, after her wont, *had* made confession of her passion for me in some private letter to her son. Was it just, Rufinus, was it consistent, I will not say with filial piety but with common humanity, that these letters should be circulated and, above all, published and proclaimed abroad by her own son? But perhaps I am no better than a fool to ask you to have regard for another's sense of decency when you have so long lost your own.

85. Why should I only complain of what is past? The present is equally distressing. To think that this unhappy boy should have been so corrupted by you as to read aloud in the proconsular court, before a man of such lofty character as Claudius Maximus, a letter from his mother, which he chooses to regard as amatory, and in the presence of the statues of the emperor Pius to accuse his mother of yielding to a shameful passion and reproach her with her *amours*? Who is there of such gentle temper, but that this would wake him to fury? Vilest of creatures, do you pry into your mother's heart in such matters, do you watch her glances, count her sighs, sound her affections, intercept her letters, and accuse her of being in love? Do you seek to discover what she does in the privacy of her own chamber, do you demand—I will not say that she should be above love affairs—but that she should cease to be a woman? Cannot you conceive the possibility that she should show any affection save the affection of a mother for her son? Ah! Pudentilla, you are unhappy in your offspring! Far better have been barren than have borne such children! Ill-omened were the long months through which you bore them in your womb and thankless your fourteen years of widowhood! The viper, I am told, reaches the light of day only by gnawing through its mother's womb; its parent must die ere it be born. But your son is full-grown and the wounds he deals are far bitterer, for they are inflicted on you while you yet live and see the light of day. He insults your reserve, he arraigns your modesty, he wounds you to the heart and outrages your dearest affections. Is this the gratitude with which a dutiful son like yourself repays his mother for the life she gave him, for the inheritance she won him, for her long fourteen years of seclusion? Is the result of your uncle's teaching this, that, if you were sure your sons would be like yourself, you should be afraid to take a wife? There is a well-known line

I hate the boy that's wise before his time.

Yes, and who would not loathe and detest a boy that is 'wicked before his time', when he sees you, like some frightful portent, old in sin but young in years, with the bodily powers of a boy, yet deep in guilt, with the bright face of a child, but with wickedness such as might match grey hairs? Nay, the most offensive thing about him is that his pernicious deeds go scot free; he is too young to punish, yet old enough to do injury. Injury, did I say? No! crime, unfilial, black, monstrous, intolerable crime!

86. The Athenians, when they captured the correspondence of their enemy, Philip of Macedon, and the letters were being read in public one by one, out of reverence for the common rights of humanity forbade one letter to be read aloud, a letter addressed by Philip to his wife Olympias. They spared the enemy that they might not intrude on the privacy of husband and wife; they placed the law that is common to all mankind above the claims of private vengeance. So enemy dealt with enemy! How have you dealt with the mother that bore you? You see how close is my parallel. Yet you read out aloud letters written by your mother which, according to your assertion, concern her love affairs, and you do so before this gathering here assembled, a gathering before which you would not dare to read the verses of some obscene poet, even if bidden to do so, but you would be restrained by some sense of shame. Nay, you would never have touched your mother's letters, had you ever been in touch with letters in the wider sense of the term. But you have also dared to submit a letter of your own to be read, a letter written about your mother in outrageously disrespectful, abusive, and unseemly language, written too at a time when you were still being brought up under her loving care. This letter you sent secretly to Pontianus, and you have now produced it to avoid the reproach of having sinned only once and to rescue so good a deed from oblivion![27] Poor fool, do you not realize that your uncle permitted you to do this, that he might clear himself in public estimation by using your letter as proof that even before you migrated to his house, even at the time when you caressed your mother with false words of love, you were already as cunning as any fox and devoid of all filial affection?

87. I cannot bring myself to believe Aemilianus such a fool as to think that the letter of a mere boy, who is also one of my accusers, could seriously tell against me.

There is also that forged letter by which they attempted to prove that I beguiled Pudentilla with flattery. I never wrote it and the forgery is not even plausible. What need had I of flattery, if I put my trust in magic? And how did they secure possession of that letter which must, as is usual in such affairs, have been sent to Pudentilla by some confidential servant? Why, again, should I write in such faulty words, such barbarous language, I whom my accusers admit to be quite at home in Greek? And why should I seek to seduce her by flattery so absurd and coarse? They themselves admit that I write amatory verse with sufficient sprightliness and skill. The explanation is obvious to every one; it is this. He who could not read the letter which Pudentilla wrote in Greek altogether too refined for his comprehension, found it easier to read this letter and set it off to greater advantage because it was his own.

One more point and I shall have said enough about the letters. Pudentilla, after writing in jest and irony those words 'Come then, while I am yet in my senses', sent for her sons and her daughter-in-law and lived with them for about two months. I beg this most dutiful of sons to tell us whether he then noticed his mother's alleged madness to have affected for the worse either her words or her deeds. Let him deny that she showed the utmost shrewdness in her examination of the accounts of the bailiffs, grooms, and shepherds, that she earnestly warned his brother Pontianus to be on his guard against the designs of Rufinus, that she rebuked him severely for having freely published the letter she had sent him without having read it honestly as it was written! Let him deny that, after what I have just related to you, his mother married me in her country house, as had been agreed some time previously!

88. The reason for our decision to be married by preference at her country house not far from Oea was to avoid a fresh concourse of citizens demanding largesse. It was but a short time before that Pudentilla had distributed 50,000 sesterces to the people on the occasion of Pontianus' marriage and this boy's assumption of the garb of manhood. We wished also to avoid the frequent and wearisome dinner-parties which custom generally imposes on newly-married couples. This is the whole reason, Aemilianus, why our marriage contract was signed not in the town but at a country house in the neighbourhood—to avoid squandering another 50,000 sesterces and to escape dining in your company or at your house. Is that sufficient? I must say that I am surprised that you object so strongly to the country house, considering that you spend most of your time in the country. The Julian marriage-law nowhere contains a clause to the effect that no man shall wed in a country house. Indeed, if you would know the truth, it is of far better omen for the expectation of offspring that one should marry one's wife in a country house in preference to the town, on rich soil in preference to barren ground, on the greensward of the meadow rather than the pavement of the market-place. She that would be a mother should marry in the very bosom of her mother, among the standing crops, on the fruitful plough-land, or she should lie beneath the elm that weds the vine, on the very lap of mother

earth, among the springing herbage, the trailing vine-shoots and the budding trees. I may add that the metaphor in <u>the line so well known in comedy</u>

That in the furrow children true be sown

bears out this view most strongly. The ancient Romans also, such as Quintius, <u>Serranus</u> and many others, were offered not only wives but consulships and dictatorships in the open field. But I am becoming long-winded. I will restrain myself for fear of gratifying you by my praise of country life.

89. As to Pudentilla's age, concerning which you lied so boldly as to assert that she had married at the age of sixty, I will reply in a few words. It is not necessary to speak at length in discussing a matter where the truth is so obvious.

Her father acknowledged her for his daughter in the usual fashion; the documents in which he did so are preserved partly in the public record office, partly in his house. Here they are before your very eyes. Please hand the documents to Aemilianus. Let him examine the linen strip that bears the seal; let him recognize the seal stamped upon it, let him read the names of the consuls for the year, let him count up the years. He gave her sixty years. Let him bring out the total at fifty-five, admitting that he lied and gave her five too many. Nay, that is hardly enough. I will deal yet more liberally with him. He gave Pudentilla such a number of years that I will reward him by returning ten. Mezentius has been wandering with Ulysses; let him at least prove that she is fifty. To cut the matter short, as I am dealing with an accuser who is used to <u>multiplying by four</u>, I will multiply five years by four and subtract twenty years at one fell swoop. I beg you, Maximus, to order the number of consuls since her birth to be reckoned. If I am not mistaken, you will find that Pudentilla has barely passed her fortieth year. The insolent audacity of this falsehood! Twenty years' exile would be a worthy punishment for such mendacity! Your fiction has added a good half to the sum, your fabrication is one and a half times the size of the original. Had you said thirty years when you ought to have said ten, it might have been supposed that you had made <u>a slip in the gesture</u> used for your calculation, that you had placed your forefinger against the middle joint of your thumb, when you should have made them form a circle. But whereas the gesture indicating forty is the simplest of all such gestures, for you have merely to hold out the palm of your hand—you have increased the number by half as much again. There is no room for an erroneous gesture; the only possible hypothesis is that, believing Pudentilla to be thirty, you got your total by adding up the number of consuls, two to each year.

90. I have done with this. I come now to the very heart of the accusation, to the actual motive for the use of magic. I ask Rufinus and Aemilianus to

answer me and tell me—even assuming that I am the most consummate magician—what had I to gain by persuading Pudentilla to marry me by means of my love philtres and my incantations. I am well aware that many persons, when accused of some crime or other, even if it has been shown that there was some real motive for the offence, have amply cleared themselves of guilt by this one line of defence, that the whole record of their lives renders the suspicion of such a crime incredible and that even though there may have been strong temptation to sin, the mere fact of the existence of the temptation should not be counted against them. We have no right to assume that everything that might have been done actually has been done. Circumstances may alter; the one true guide is a man's character; the one sure indication that a charge should be rejected or believed is the fact that through all his life the accused has set his face towards vice or virtue as the case may be. I might with the utmost justice put in such a plea for myself, but I waive my right in your favour, and shall think that I have made out but a poor case for myself, if I do no more than amply clear myself of all your charges and show that there exists not the slightest ground for suspecting me of sorcery. Consider what confidence in my innocence and what contempt of you is implied by my conduct. If you can discover one trivial reason that might have led me to woo Pudentilla for the sake of some personal advantage, if you can prove that I have made the very slightest profit out of my marriage, I am ready to be any magician you please—the great [Carmendas himself or Damigeron](#) or Moses[28] of whom you have heard, or Jannes or Apollobex or Dardanus himself or any sorcerer of note from the time of Zoroaster and Ostanes till now.

91. See, Maximus, what a disturbance they have raised, merely because I have mentioned a few magicians by name. What am I to do with men so stupid and uncivilized? Shall I proceed to prove to you that I have come across these names and many more in the course of my study of distinguished authors in the public libraries? Or shall I argue that the knowledge of the names of sorcerers is one thing, participation in their art another, and that it is not tantamount to confessing a crime to have one's brain well stored with learning and a memory retentive of its erudition? Or shall I take what is far the best course and, relying on your learning, Maximus, and your perfect erudition, disdain to reply to the accusations of these stupid and uncultivated fellows? Yes, that is what I will do. I will not care a straw for what they may think. I will go on with the argument on which I had entered and will show that I had no motive for seducing Pudentilla into marriage by the use of love philtres.

My accusers have gone out of their way to make disparaging remarks both about her age and her appearance; they have denounced me for desiring such a wife from motives of greed and robbing her of her vast and magnificent dowry at the very outset of our wedded life. I do not intend to weary you, Maximus, with a long reply on these points. There is no need for words from me, our deeds of settlement will speak more eloquently than I can do. From them you will see that both in my provision for the future and in my action at the time my conduct was precisely the opposite of that which they have attributed to me, inferring my rapacity from their own. You will see that Pudentilla's dowry was small, considering her wealth, and was made over to me as a trust not as a gift, and moreover that the marriage only took place on this condition that if my wife should die without leaving me any children, the dowry should go to her sons Pontianus and Pudens, while if at her death she should leave me one son or daughter, half of the dowry was to go to the offspring of the second marriage, the remainder to the sons of the first.

92. This, as I say, I will prove from the actual deed of settlement. It may be that Aemilianus will still refuse to believe that the total sum recorded is only 300,000 sesterces, and that the reversion of this sum is given by the settlement to Pudentilla's sons. Take the deeds into your own hands, give them to Rufinus who incited you to this accusation. Let him read them, let him blush for his arrogant temper and his pretentious beggary. *He* is poor and ill-clad and borrowed 400,000 sesterces to dower his daughter, while Pudentilla, a woman of fortune, was content with 300,000, and her husband, who has often refused the hand of the richest heiresses, is also content with this trifling dowry, a mere nominal sum. He cares for nothing save his wife and counts the mutual love and harmony of his wedded life as his sole treasure, his only wealth. Who that had the least experience of life, would dare to pass any censure if a widow of inconsiderable beauty and considerable age, being desirous of marriage, had by the offer of a large dowry and easy conditions invited a young man, who, whether as regards appearance, character or wealth, was no despicable match, to become her husband? A beautiful maiden, even though she be poor, is amply dowered. For she brings to her husband a fresh untainted spirit, the charm of her beauty, the unblemished glory of her prime. The very fact that she is a maiden is rightly and deservedly regarded by all husbands as the strongest recommendation. For whatever else you receive as your wife's dowry you can, when it pleases you and if you desire to feel yourself under no further obligation, repay in full just as you received it; you can count back the money, restore the slaves, leave the house, abandon the estates. Virginity only, once it has been given, can never be repaid; it is the one portion of the dowry that remains irrevocably with the husband. A widow on the other hand, if divorced, leaves you as she came. She brings you nothing that she cannot ask back, she has been another's and is certainly far from tractable to your wishes; she looks suspiciously on her new home, while you regard her with suspicion because she has already been parted from one husband: if it was by death she lost her husband, the evil omen of her ill-starred union minimizes her

attractions, while, if she left him by divorce, she possesses one of two faults: either she was so intolerable that she was divorced by her husband, or so insolent as to divorce him. It is for reasons of this kind among others that widows offer a larger dowry to attract suitors for their hands. Pudentilla would have done the same had she not found a philosopher indifferent to her dowry.

93. Consider. If I had desired her from motives of avarice, what could have been more profitable to me in my attempt to make myself master in her house than the dissemination of strife between mother and sons, the alienation of her children from her affections, so that I might have unfettered and supreme control over her loneliness? Such would have been, would it not, the action of the brigand you pretend me to be. But as a matter of fact I did all I could to promote, to restore and foster quiet and harmony and family affection, and not only abstained from sowing fresh feuds, but utterly extinguished those already in existence. I urged my wife—whose whole fortune according to my accusers I had by this time devoured—I urged her and finally persuaded her, when her sons demanded back the money of which I spoke above, to pay over the whole sum at once in the shape of farms, at a low valuation and at the price suggested by themselves, and further to surrender from her own private property certain exceedingly fertile lands, a large house richly decorated, a great quantity of wheat, barley, wine and oil, and other fruits of the earth, together with not less than four hundred slaves and a large number of valuable cattle. Finally I persuaded her to abandon all claims on the portion she had given them and to give them good hopes of one day coming into the rest of the property. All these concessions I extorted from Pudentilla with difficulty and against her will—I have her leave to tell the whole story as it happened—I wrung them from her by my urgent entreaty, though she was angry and reluctant. I reconciled the mother with her sons, and began my career as a step-father by enriching my stepsons with a large sum of money.

94. All Oea was aware of this. Every one execrated Rufinus and extolled my conduct. Pontianus together with his very inferior brother had come to visit us, before his mother had completed her donation. He fell at our feet and implored us to forgive and forget all his past offences; he wept, kissed our hands and expressed his penitence for listening to Rufinus and others like him. He also most humbly begged me to make his excuses to the most honourable Lollianus Avitus to whom I had recommended him not long before when he was beginning the study of oratory. He had discovered that I had written to Avitus a few days previously a full account of all that had happened. I granted him this request also and gave him a letter with which he set off to Carthage, where Lollianus Avitus, the term of his proconsulate having nearly expired, was awaiting your arrival, Maximus. After reading my

letters he congratulated Pontianus with the exquisite courtesy which always characterizes him for having so soon rectified his error and entrusted him with a reply. Ah! what learning! what wit! what grace and charm dwelt in that reply! Only a 'good man and an orator' could have written it. I know, Maximus, that you will readily give a hearing to this letter. Indeed, if it is to be read, I will recite it myself. Give me Avitus' letter. That I should have received it has always flattered me. To-day it shall do more than flatter, it shall save me! You may let the water-clock continue, for I would gladly read and re-read the letter of that excellent man to the third and fourth time at the cost of any amount of the time allowed me. (*The letter is read.*)

95. I know that after reading this letter I should bring my speech to a close. For what ampler commendation, what purer testimony could I produce in my support, what more eloquent advocacy? I have in the course of my life listened with rapt attention to many eloquent Romans, but never have I admired any so much as Avitus. There is in my opinion no one living of any attainments or promise in oratory who would not far sooner be Avitus, if he compare him with himself impartially and without envy. For practically all the different excellencies of oratory are united in him. Whatever speech Avitus composes will be found so absolutely perfect and complete in all respects that it would satisfy Cato by its dignity, Laelius with its smoothness, Gracchus with its energy, Caesar with its warmth, Hortensius with its arrangement, Calvus with its point, Sallust with its economy and Cicero with its wealth of rhetoric. In fact, not to go through all his merits, if you were to hear Avitus, you would wish nothing added, withdrawn or altered of anything that he says.

I see, Maximus, with what pleasure you listen to the recital of the virtues which you recognize your friend Avitus to possess. Your courtesy invited me to say a few words about him. But I will not trespass on your kindness so far as to permit myself to commence a discourse on his extraordinary virtues at this period of the case. It is wearing to its end and my powers are almost exhausted. I will rather reserve the praise of Avitus' virtues for some day when my time is free and my powers unimpaired.

96. *Now*, I grieve to say, it is my duty to turn from the description of so great a man to discuss these pestilent fellows here.

Do you dare then, Aemilianus, to match yourself against Avitus? Will you attack with accusations of magic and the black art him whom Avitus describes as a good man, and whose disposition he praises so warmly in his letter? Or have you greater reason to be vexed at my forcing my way into Pudentilla's house and pillaging her goods than Pontianus would have had, Pontianus, who not only in my presence but even before Avitus in my absence, made amends for the strife of a few days that had sprung up between us at your instigation, and expressed his gratitude to me in the presence of so great a man? Suppose I had read a report of what took place in Avitus' presence instead of reading merely his letter. What is there in the whole affair that could give you or any one else[29] a handle for accusing me? Pontianus himself considered himself in my debt for the money given him by his mother; Pontianus rejoiced with the utmost sincerity in his good fortune in having me for his step-father. Ah! would that he had returned from Carthage safe and sound! or since it was not fated that that should be, would that you, Rufinus, had not poisoned his judgement at the last! What gratitude he would have expressed to me either personally or in his will! However, as things are, I beg you, Maximus,—it will not take long—to allow the reading of these letters full of expressions of respect and affection for myself, which he sent me, some of them from Carthage, some as he drew near on his homeward journey, some written while he still enjoyed his health, and some when the sickness was already upon him. Thus his brother, my accuser, will realize with what[30] lack of success he pursues his literary studies compared with his brother of blessed memory. (*Pontianus' letters are read.*)

97. Did you hear the phrases which your brother Pontianus used in speaking of me? He called me his father, his master, his instructor not only on various occasions in his lifetime but actually on his deathbed. I might follow this[31] by producing similar letters from you, if I thought that the delay thus caused would be worth while. But I should prefer to produce your brother's recent will, unfinished though it may be, in which he made most dutiful and respectful mention of myself. But Rufinus never allowed this will to be drawn up or completed owing to his chagrin at the loss of the inheritance which he had regarded in the light of a rich payment[32] for his daughter's embraces during the few months in which he was Pontianus' father-in-law. He had further consulted certain Chaldean soothsayers as to what profit his daughter, whom he regarded in the light of an investment, would bring him in. They, I am told, prophesied truly—would they had not—that her first husband would die in a few months. The rest of the prophecy dealing with the inheritance was as usual fabricated to suit the desires of their client. But Rufinus gaped for his prey in vain like a wild beast that has gone blind. For Pontianus not only did not leave Rufinus' daughter as his heir—he had discovered her evil character—but he did not even make her a respectable legacy. He left her by way of insult linen to the value of 200 denarii, to show that he had not forgotten or ignored her, but that he set this value on her as an expression of his resentment. As his heirs—in this just as in the former will which has been read aloud—he appointed his mother and his brother, against whom, mere boy as he is, Rufinus is, as you see, bringing his old artillery into play: I refer to his daughter. He thrusts her upon his embraces

although she is considerably his elder and but a brief while ago was his brother's wife.

98. Pudens was so captivated and possessed by the charms of that harlot and by the beguiling words of the pander, her father, that the moment his brother had breathed his last, he left his mother and migrated to his uncle's house. The design was to facilitate the carrying out of the schemes already afoot by removing him from our influence. For Aemilianus is backing Rufinus and desires his success. (*A movement among the audience.*) Ah! Thank you! You rightly remind me that this excellent uncle has hopes of his own mixed up in this affair, for he knows that if this boy dies intestate he will be his heir-at-law, whatever he may be in point of equity. I wish I had not let this slip. I am a man of great self-control and it is not my way to blurt out openly the silent suspicions that must have occurred to every one. You did wrong in suggesting this point to me. But to be frank, if you will have the truth, many have been wondering at the sudden affection which you, Aemilianus, have begun to show for this boy since the death of his brother Pontianus, whereas formerly you were such a stranger to him that frequently, even when you met him, you failed to recognize the face of your brother's son. But now you show yourself so patient towards him, you so spoil him by your indulgence and grant his every whim to such an extent that your conduct makes the more suspicious think their suspicions well grounded. You took him from us a mere boy and straightway gave him the garb of manhood. While he was under our guardianship, he used to go to school: now he has bidden a long farewell to study and betaken himself to the delights of the tavern. He despises serious friends, and, boy as he is, spends his tender years in revelling with the most abandoned youths among harlots and wine-cups. He rules your house, orders your slaves, directs your banquets. He is a frequent visitor to the gladiatorial school and there—as a boy of position should!—he learns from the keeper of the school the names of the gladiators, the fights they have fought, the wounds they have received. He never speaks any language save Punic, and though he may occasionally use a Greek word picked up from his mother, he neither will nor can speak Latin. You heard, Maximus, a little while ago, you heard my step-son—oh! the shame of it!—the brother of that eloquent young fellow Pontianus, hardly able to stammer out single syllables, when you asked him whether his mother had given himself and his brother the gifts which, as I told you just now, she actually gave them with my hearty support.

99. I call you, therefore, Claudius Maximus, and you, gentlemen, his assessors, and you that with me stand before this tribunal, to bear witness that this boy's disgraceful falling away in morals is due to his uncle here and that candidate for the privilege of becoming his father-in-law, and that I shall henceforth count it a blessing that such a step-son has lifted the burden of

superintending him from my shoulders, and that from this day forth I will never intercede for him with his mother. For recently—I had almost forgotten to mention it—when Pudentilla, who had fallen ill after the death of her son Pontianus, was writing her will, I had a prolonged struggle to prevent her disinheriting this boy on account of the outrageous insult and injury he had inflicted on her. I prayed her with the utmost earnestness to erase that most important clause, which, I can assure you, she had already written, every word of it! Finally, I even threatened to leave her, if she refused to accede to my request, and begged her to grant me this boon, to conquer her wicked son by kindness, and to save me from all the ill feeling which her action would create. I did not desist till she complied. I regret that I should have smoothed Aemilianus' way for him and showed him such an unexpected path[33] to wealth. Look, Maximus, see how confused he is at hearing this, see how he casts his eyes upon the ground. He had not unnaturally expected something very different. He knew that my wife was angry with her son on account of his insolent behaviour and that she returned my devotion. He had reason also for fear in regard to myself; for any one else, even if like myself he had been above coveting the inheritance, would gladly have seen so undutiful a step-son punished. It was this anxiety above all others that spurred them on to accuse me. Their own avarice led them falsely to conjecture that the whole inheritance had been left to me. As far as the past is concerned, I will dispel your fears on that point. I was proof against the temptation both of enriching myself and of revenging myself. I—a step-father, mind you—contended for my wicked step-son with his mother, as a father might contend against a stepmother in the interests of a virtuous son; nor did I rest satisfied till, with a perfectly extravagant sense of fairness, I had restrained my good wife's lavish generosity towards myself.

100. Give me the will which was made in the interests of so unfilial a son by his mother. Each word of it was preceded by an entreaty from myself, whom my accusers speak of as a mere robber. Order the tablets to be broken open, Maximus. You will find that her son is the heir, that I get nothing save some trifling complimentary legacy inserted to avoid the non-appearance of my name, the husband's name, mark you, in my wife's will, supposing she succumbed to any of the ills to which this flesh is heir. Take up your mother's will. You are right, in one respect it is undutiful. She excludes her devoted husband from the inheritance in favour of her most unfilial son? Nay, it is not her son to whom she leaves her fortune; she leaves it rather to the greedy Aemilianus and the matchmaking Rufinus and that drunken gang, that hang about you and prey upon you. Take it, O best of sons! Lay aside your mother's love-letters for a while and read her will instead. If she ever wrote anything while not in her right mind, you will find it here, nor will you have to go far to find it. 'Let Sicinius Pudens, my son, be my heir.' I admit it! he who reads this, will think it insanity. Is this same son your heir, who at his

own brother's funeral attempted with the help of a gang of the most abandoned youths to shut you out of the house which you yourself had given him, who is so deeply and bitterly incensed to find that his brother left you co-heir with himself, who hastened to desert you when you were plunged in grief and mourning, and fled from your bosom to Aemilianus and Rufinus, who afterwards uttered many insults against you to your face, and manufactured others with the help of his uncle, who has dragged your name through the law-courts, has attempted by using your own letters publicly to besmirch your fair fame, and has accused upon a capital charge the husband of your choice, with whom, as Pudens himself objected, you were madly in love! Open the will, my good boy, open it, I beg you. You will find it easier then to prove your mother's insanity.

Why do you draw back? Why do you refuse to look at it, now that you are free from all anxiety about the inheritance of your mother's fortune?

101. He may do as he likes, Maximus, but for my part I cast these tablets at your feet and call you to witness that henceforth I shall show greater indifference as to what Pudentilla may write in her will. He may approach his mother himself for the future; he has made it impossible for me to plead for him again. He is now a man and his own master; henceforth let him himself dictate to his mother the terms[34] of an unpalatable will, himself smooth away her anger. He who can plead in court, will be able to plead with his mother. I am more than satisfied not only to have refuted the miscellaneous accusations brought against myself, but also to have utterly swept away the hateful charge on which the whole trial is based, the charge of having attempted to secure the inheritance for myself.

I will bring one final proof to show the falsity of that last charge before I bring my speech to a close. I wish to pass nothing over in silence. You asserted that I bought a most excellent farm in my own name, but with a large sum of money which belonged to my wife. I say that a tiny property was bought for 60,000 sesterces, and bought not by me but by Pudentilla in her own name, that Pudentilla's name is in the deed of sale, and that the taxes paid on the land are paid in the name of Pudentilla. The honourable Corvinus Celer, the state treasurer to whom the tax is paid, is here in court. Cassius Longinus also is present, my wife's guardian and trustee, a man of the loftiest and most irreproachable character. I cannot speak of him save with the deepest respect. Ask him, Maximus, what was the purchase which he authorized, and what was the trifling sum for which this wealthy lady bought her little estate. (*Cassius Longinus and Corvinus Celer give evidence.*)

Is it as I said? Is my name ever mentioned in the deed of sale? Is the price paid for this trifling property such as should excite any prejudice against me, or did my wife give me even so much as this small gift?

102. What is there left, Aemilianus, that in your opinion I have failed to refute? What had I to gain by my magic that should lead me to attempt to win Pudentilla by love-philtres? What had I to gain from her? A small dowry instead of a large one? Truly my incantations were miraculous. That she should refund her dowry to her sons rather than leave it in my possession? What magic can surpass this? That she should at my exhortation present the bulk of her property to her sons and leave me nothing, although before her marriage with myself she had shown them no special generosity? <u>What a criminal use of love-philtres!</u> or perhaps I had better call it a generous action which has not received its deserts! By her will, which she drew up in a fit of violent irritation against her son, she leaves as her heir that same son with whom she had quarrelled, rather than myself to whom she was devoted! For all my incantations it was only with difficulty that I persuaded her to this. Suppose that you were pleading your case, not before Claudius Maximus, a man of the utmost fairness and unswerving justice, but before a judge of depraved morals and of ferocious temper, one in fact who naturally inclined to the side of the accuser and was only too ready to condemn the accused! Give him some hint to follow! Give him even the slightest reasonable opportunity for declaring in your favour! At least invent something, devise some suitable reply to questions such as have been put to you. Nay, since every action must necessarily have some motive, answer me this, you who say that Apuleius tried to influence Pudentilla's heart by magical charms, answer me this! What did he seek to get from her by so doing? Was he in love with her beauty? You say not! Did he covet her wealth? The evidence of the marriage settlement denies it, the evidence of the deed of gift denies it, the evidence of the will denies it! It shows not only that I did not court the generosity of my wife, but that I even repulsed it with some severity. What other motives can you allege? Why are you struck dumb? Why this silence? What has become of that ferocious utterance with which you opened the indictment, couched in the name of my step-son? 'This is the man, most excellent Maximus, whom I have resolved to indict before you.'

103. Why did you not add 'He whom I indict is my teacher, my step-father, my mediator'? But how did you proceed? 'He is guilty of the most palpable and numerous sorceries.' Produce one of these many sorceries or at least some doubtful instance from those which you style so palpable. Nay, see whether I cannot reply to your various charges with two words to each. 'You clean your teeth.' Excusable cleanliness. 'You look into mirrors.' Philosophers should. 'You write verse.' 'Tis permitted. 'You examine fish.' Following Aristotle. 'You worship a piece of wood.' So Plato. 'You marry a wife.' Obeying law. 'She is older than you.' Nothing commoner. 'You married for money.' Take the marriage-settlement, remember the deed of gift, read the will!

If I have rebutted all their charges, word by word, if I have refuted all their slanders, if I am beyond reproach, not only as regards their accusations but also as regards their vulgar abuse, if I have done nothing to impair the honour of philosophy, which is dearer to me than my own safety, but on the contrary have smitten my adversary hip and thigh and vanquished him at all points, if all my contentions are true, I can await your estimate of my character with the same confidence with which I await the exercise of your power; for I regard it as less serious and less terrible to be condemned by the proconsul than to incur the disapproval of so good and so perfect a man.

THE FLORIDA

The exordium to a discourse delivered in a town through which Apuleius passes in the course of a journey.

1. It is the usual practice of wayfarers with a religious disposition, when they come upon a sacred grove or holy place by the roadside, to utter a prayer, to offer an apple, and pause for a moment from their journeying. So I, on entering the revered walls of your city, feel that, for all my haste, it is my duty to ask your favour, to make an address, and to break the speed of my journey. I cannot conceive aught that could give a traveller juster cause to halt in sign of reverence; no altar crowned with flowers, no grotto shadowed with foliage,[35] no oak bedecked with horns, no beech garlanded with the skins of beasts, no mound whose engirdling hedge proclaims its sanctity, no tree-trunk hewn into the semblance of a god, no turf still wet with libations, no stone astream with precious unguents. For these are but small things, and though there be a few that seek them out and do them worship, the majority note them not and pass them by.

Man's sight compared with that of the eagle.

2. But such was not the opinion of my master Socrates. For once when he saw a youth of handsome appearance who remained for a long time without uttering a syllable, he said to him, 'Say something, that I may see what you are like.' For Socrates felt that a man who spoke not at all was in a sense invisible, since he held that it was not with the bodily vision, but with the mind's eye and the sight of the soul that men should be regarded. In this he disagreed with the soldier in Plautus, who says,

One man that has eyes is better by far as a witness than ten that have ears.

Indeed, for the purpose of examining men he had practically reversed the meaning of the line to

One man that has ears is better by far as a witness than ten that have eyes.

Moreover, if the judgements of the eye were of greater value than those of the soul, we should assuredly have to yield the palm for wisdom to the eagle. For we men cannot see things far removed from us nor yet things that are very near us, but all of us to a certain extent are blind. And if you confine us to the eyes alone with their dim earthly vision, the words of the great poet will be very true, that a cloud as it were is shed upon our eyes and we cannot see beyond a stone's cast. The eagle, on the other hand, soars exceeding high in heaven to the very clouds, and rides on his pinions through all that space where there is rain and snow, regions beyond whose heights thunderbolts and lightnings have no place, even to the very floor of heaven and the topmost verge of the storms of earth. And having towered thus high, with gentle motion he turns his great body to glide to left or right, directing his wings, that are as sails, whither he will by the movement of his tail, which, small though it be, serves as a rudder. Thence he gazes down on the world, staying awhile in that far height[36] the ceaseless oarage of his wings and, poised almost motionless with hovering flight, looks all around him and seeks what prey he shall choose whereon to swoop[37] sudden like a thunderbolt from heaven on high. In one glance he sees all cattle in the field, all beasts upon the mountains, all men in their cities, all threatened at once by his intended swoop, and thence he falls to pierce with his beak and clutch with his claws the unsuspecting lamb, the timid hare, or whatsoever living creature chance offers to his hunger or his talons.

The story of Marsyas and his challenge to Apollo.

3. Hyagnis, according to tradition, was the father and instructor of the piper Marsyas, and skilled in song beyond all others in the years when music was still in its infancy. It is true that as yet the sound of his breath lacked the finer modulations; he knew but a few simple modes and his pipe had but few stops. For the art was but newly born and only just beginning to grow. There is nothing that can attain perfection in its first beginnings; everything must commence by mastering the elements in hope, ere it can attain experience and success. Well, then, before Hyagnis the majority of musicians could do no more than the shepherds or cowherds of Vergil who

Made sorry strains on pipes of scrannel straw.

If any of them seemed to have made some real advance in art, even he played only on one pipe or one trumpet. Hyagnis was the first to separate his hands when he played, the first to fill two pipes with one breath, the first to finger stops with either hand and make sweet harmony of shrill treble and booming bass. Marsyas was his son, and though he possessed his father's skill upon the pipe, he was in all else a barbarous Phrygian, with a filthy beard and the grim and shaggy face of a wild beast. All his body was covered with hair and bristles, and yet—good heavens! he is said to have striven for mastery with Apollo. 'Twas hideousness contending with beauty, a rude boor against a sage, a beast against a god. The Muses and Minerva, hiding their amusement, stood by to judge, that they might make a mockery of the monster's uncouth presumption and punish his stupidity. But Marsyas, like the peerless fool he was, never perceived that he was an object of ridicule, and before he began to blow upon his pipes stammered out in his barbarous jargon some insane boasts about himself and Apollo. He prided himself on the mane thrown back from his brow, on his unkempt beard, his shaggy breast, his skill upon the pipes and his lack of wealth. By contrast—oh the absurdity of it!—he blamed Apollo for the opposite of these qualities, for being Apollo, for wearing his hair long, for having a fair face and smooth body, for his skill in so many arts, and for the opulence of his fortune. 'In the first place,' he said, 'his hair is smoothed and plastered into tufts and curls that fall about his brow and hang before his face. His body is fair from head to foot, his limbs shine bright, his tongue gives oracles, and he is equally eloquent in prose or verse, propose which you will. What of his robes so fine in texture, so soft to the touch, aglow with purple? What of his lyre that flashes gold, gleams white with ivory, and shimmers with rainbow gems? What of his song, so cunning and so sweet? Nay, all these allurements suit with naught save luxury. To virtue they bring shame alone!' And then he proceeded to display his own body as the model of perfection. The Muses laughed when they heard him denounce Apollo for possessing gifts such as the wise would pray to possess, and when this boastful piper had been defeated in the contest and had been skinned as though he were a two-footed bear, they left him with his entrails torn and exposed to the air. Thus did Marsyas sing for his own undoing, and such was his fall. As for Apollo he was ashamed of so inglorious a victory.

The piper Antigenidas.

4. There was a certain piper named Antigenidas, whose every note made honeyed harmony. He had skill, too, to make music in every mode, choose which you would, the simple Aeolian or the complex Ionian, the mournful Lydian, the solemn Phrygian, or the warlike Dorian. Being therefore the most famous of all that played upon the pipe, he said that nothing so tormented him, nothing so vexed his heart and soul, as the fact that the musicians who played the trumpet at funerals were dignified by the name of pipers. But he would have endured this identity of names with equanimity, had he ever seen the performance of mimes; for he would have noted that the magistrates, who preside in the theatre, and the characters on the stage, who come in for a good cudgelling, are clad in practically the same purple garments. So too, had he ever watched our games! For he would have seen one presiding, another fighting, yet both of them sharing the same common humanity. He would have noted that the Roman toga is worn alike by him who performs a vow to heaven and by him that lies dead upon the bier, that the Grecian pallium serves to shroud the dead no less than to clothe the philosopher.

Fragment from the opening of a discourse delivered in a theatre.

5. You have, I feel assured, come to this theatre with the best will in the world. For you know that the importance of an oration does not depend on the place in which it is delivered, but that the first thing that has to be considered is, 'What form of entertainment is the theatre going to provide?'

If it is a mime, you will laugh; if a rope-walker, you will tremble lest he fall; if a comedian, you will applaud him, while, if it be a philosopher, you will learn from him.

India and the Gymnosophists.

5. India is a populous country of enormous extent. It lies far to the east of us, close to the point where ocean turns back upon himself and the sun rises, on that verge where meet the last of lands and the first stars of heaven. Far away it lies, beyond the learned Egyptians, beyond the superstitious Jews and the merchants of Nabataea, beyond the children of Arsaces in their long flowing robes, the Ityreans, to whom earth gives but scanty harvest, and the Arabs, whose perfumes are their wealth. Wherefore I marvel not so much at the great stores of ivory possessed by these Indians, their harvests of pepper, their exports of cinnamon, their finely-tempered steel, their mines of silver and their rivers of gold. I marvel not so much that in the Ganges they have the greatest of all rivers which

Lord of all the waters of the East
Is cloven and parted in a hundred streams.
A hundred vales are his, a hundred mouths,
And hundred-fold the flood that meets the main;

nor wonder I that the Indians that dwell at the very portals of day are yet of the hue of night, nor that in their land vast serpents engage in combat with huge elephants, to the equal danger and the common destruction of either; for they envelop and bind their prey in slippery coils so that they cannot disengage their feet nor in any wise break the scaly fetters of these clinging snakes, but must needs find vengeance by hurling their vast bulk to the ground and crushing the foe that grips them by the weight of their whole bodies. But it is of the marvels of men rather than of nature that I would speak.[38] For the dwellers in this land are divided into many castes. There is one whose sole skill lies in tending herds of oxen, whence they are known as the oxherds. There are others who are cunning in the barter of merchandise, others who are sturdy warriors in battle and have skill to fight at long range with arrows or hand to hand with swords. There is, further, one caste that is especially remarkable. They are called gymnosophists. At these I marvel most of all. For they are skilled—not in growing the vine, or grafting fruit-trees, or ploughing the soil. They know not how to till the fields, or wash gold, or break horses, or tame bulls, or to clip or feed sheep or goats. What, then, is their claim to distinction? This: one thing they know outweighing all they know not. They honour wisdom one and all, the old that teach and the young that learn. Nor is there aught I more commend in them than that they hate that their minds should be sluggish and idle. And so, when the table is set in its place, before the viands are served, all the youths leave their homes and professions to flock to the banquet. The masters ask each one of them what good deed he has performed between the rising of the sun and the present hour. Thereupon one tells how he has been chosen as arbiter between two of his fellows, has healed their quarrel, reconciled their strife, dispelled their suspicions and made them friends instead of foes. Another tells how he has obeyed some command of his parents, another relates some discovery that his meditations have brought him or some new knowledge won from another's exposition. And so with the rest of them,[39] they tell their story. He who can give no good reason for joining in the feast is thrust fasting from the doors to go to his work.

On Alexander and false philosophers.

7. The famous Alexander, by far the noblest of all kings, won the title of the Great from the deeds that he had done and the empire he had built, and thus it was secured that the man who had won glory without peer should never be so much as named without a word of praise. For he alone since time began, alone of all whereof man's memory bears record, after he had conquered a world-wide empire such as none may ever surpass, proved himself greater than his fortune. By his energy he challenged the most glorious successes that fortune could bestow, equalled them by his worth, surpassed them by his virtues, and stood alone in peerless glory, so that none might dare even hope for such virtue or pray for such fortune. The life of this Alexander is marked by so many lofty deeds and glorious acts, be it of prowess in the battle or statecraft in the council chamber, that you may marvel at them till you are weary. It is the story of all these great achievements that my friend Clemens, most learned and sweetest of poets, has attempted to glorify in the exquisite strains of his verse.

Now among the most remarkable acts recorded of Alexander is this. Desiring that his likeness should be handed down to posterity with as little variation as possible, he refused to permit it to be profaned by a multitude of artists, and issued a proclamation to all the world over which he ruled that no one should rashly counterfeit the king's likeness in bronze or with the painter's colours, or with the sculptor's chisel. Only Polycletus might portray him in bronze, only Apelles depict him in colour, only Pyrgoteles carve his form with the engraver's chisel. If any other than these three, each supreme in his peculiar art, should be discovered to have set his hand to reproduce the sacred image of the king, he should be punished as severely as though he had committed sacrilege. This order struck such fear into all men that Alexander alone of mankind was always like his portraits, and that every statue, painting, or bronze revealed the same fierce martial vigour, the same great and glorious genius, the same fresh and youthful beauty, the same fair forehead with its back-streaming hair. And would that philosophy could issue a like proclamation that should have equal weight, forbidding unauthorized persons to reproduce her likeness; then the study and contemplation of wisdom in all her aspects would be in the hands of a few good craftsmen who had been carefully trained, and unlettered fellows of base life and little learning would ape the philosopher no longer (though their imitation does not go beyond <u>the professor's gown</u>), and the queen of all studies, whose aim is no less excellence of speech than excellence of life, would no longer be profaned by evil speech and evil living: and, mark you, profanation of either kind is far from hard. What is more readily come by than madness of speech and worthlessness of character? The former springs from contempt of others, the latter from contempt of self. For to show little care for one's own character is self-contempt, while to attack others with uncouth and savage speech is an insult to those that hear you. For is it not the height of insolence, think you, that a man should deem you to rejoice in hearing abuse of the best of men, and should believe that you do not understand evil and wicked words, or, if you do understand them, hold them to be good? What boor, what porter, what taverner is so poor of speech that could not curse more eloquently than these folk, if he would consent to assume the professor's gown?

A eulogy of the proconsul of Africa.

8. He owes more to his personal character than to his rank, although even his rank is one that is shared by few. For out of numberless multitudes of men not many are senators, of senators but few are of noble birth, of the noble but few attain to the rank of consul, of consuls but few are good, and of the good but few are learned. But to confine what I have to say to his high office, 'tis not lightly that any man may assume the insignia of his rank either as regards clothing or foot-gear.

A defence of himself against his critics and a laudation of the proconsul Severianus.

9. If it should so chance that in this magnificent gathering there should sit any of those that envy or hate me, since in a great city persons may always be found who prefer to abuse rather than imitate persons better than themselves, and, since they cannot be like them, affect to hate them. They do this of course in order to illumine the obscurity that shrouds their own names by the splendour that falls from mine; if then, I say, any one of these envious persons sullies this distinguished audience with the stain of his presence, I would ask him for a moment to cast his eyes round this incredibly vast concourse. When he has contemplated a throng such as before my day never yet gathered to listen to a philosopher, let him consider in his heart how great a risk to his reputation is undertaken by a man who is not used to contempt in appearing here to-day; for it is an arduous task, and far from easy of accomplishment, to satisfy even the moderate expectations of a few.

Above all it is difficult for me, for the fame I have already won and your own kindly anticipation of my skill will not permit me to deliver any ill-considered or superficial utterance. For what man among you would pardon me one solecism or condone the barbarous pronunciation of so much as one syllable? Who of you will suffer me to stammer in disorderly and faulty phrases such as might rise to the lips of madmen? In others of course you would pardon such lapses, and very rightly so. But you subject every word that *I* utter to the closest examination, you weigh it carefully, you try it by the plumb-line and the file, you test it by the polish of the lathe and the sublimity of the tragic buskin. Such is the indulgence accorded to mediocrity, such the severity meted out to distinction. I recognize, therefore, the difficulty of the task that lies before me, and I do not ask you to alter the opinions you entertain of me. Yet I would not have you deceived by false and petty resemblances, for, as I have often said, there are certain strolling beggars who assume a professor's gown to win their livelihood. Not only the proconsul, but the town crier also ascends the tribunal and appears wearing the toga like his master. But the crier stands upon his feet for hours together, or strides to and fro, or bawls his news with all the strength of his lungs. The proconsul, on the contrary, speaks quietly and with frequent pauses, sits while he speaks, and often reads from a written document. This is only natural. For the garrulous voice of the crier is the voice of a hired servant, the words read by the proconsul from a written document constitute a judgement, which, once read, may not have one letter added to it or taken away, but so soon as it is delivered, is set down in the provincial records. My literary position will provide a humble analogy. All that I utter before you is forthwith taken down and read. I can withdraw or change nothing, nor make the least correction. I must therefore be all the more careful in what I say before you, and that too with regard to more than one form of composition. For there is greater variety in the works of my muse than in all the elaborate achievements of Hippias. If you will give me your best attention I will explain what I mean with greater detail and precision.

Hippias was one of the sophists, and surpassed all his fellows in the variety of his accomplishments, while as an orator he was second to none. He was a contemporary of Socrates, and a native of Elis. Of his family nothing is known. But his fame was great, his fortune moderate; moreover he had a noble wk and an extraordinary memory, pursued many branches of study, and had many rivals. This Hippias, of whom I speak, once came to Pisa during the Olympian games arrayed in raiment that was as remarkable to the eye as it was wonderful in its workmanship. For he had purchased nothing of what he wore: it was all the work of his own hands, the clothes in which he was clad, the shoes wherewith he was shod, and the jewels that made him conspicuous. Next his skin he wore an undershirt of triple weft and the finest texture, double dyed with purple. He had woven it for himself in his own house with his own hands. He had for girdle a belt, broidered in Babylonian fashion with many varied colours. In this also no man else had helped him. For outer garment he had a white cloak cast about his shoulders; this cloak also is known to have been the work of his own hands. He had fashioned even the shoes that covered his feet and the ring of gold with its cunningly engraved signet which he displayed on his left hand. Himself he had wrought the circle of gold, had closed the bezel around the gem and engraved the stone. I have not yet told you all the tale of his achievements. But I will not shrink from enumerating all the marvels that he thought it no shame to show. For he proclaimed before that vast concourse that his own hands had fashioned the oil-flask which he carried. It was in shape a flattened sphere, and its outlines were round and smooth. Beside it he showed an exquisite flesh-scraper, the handle[40] of which was straight, while the tongue was curved and grooved with hollow channels, so that the hand might have a firm grip and the sweat might be carried off in a trickling stream from the blade. Who could withhold praise from a man who had such manifold knowledge of so many arts, who had won such glory in every branch of knowledge, who was, in fact, a very Daedalus,[41] such skill had he to fashion so many useful instruments? Nay, I myself praise Hippias, but I prefer to imitate his fertile genius in respect of the learning, rather than of the furniture with which it was so richly equipped. I have, I confess, but indifferent skill in these sedentary arts. When I want clothes I buy them from the weaver, when I want sandals, such as I am now wearing, I purchase them from the shoemaker. I do not carry a ring, since I regard gold and precious stones of as little value as pebbles or lead. As for flesh-scrapers and oil-flasks and other utensils of the bath I procure them in the market. I will not go to the extent of denying that I am wholly ignorant how to use a shuttle, an awl, a file, a lathe, and other tools of the kind, but I confess that I infinitely prefer to all these instruments one simple pen, with which I may write poems of all kinds, such as may suit with the reciter's wand and the accompaniment of the lyre or grace the comic or the tragic stage. Satires also do I write and riddles, histories also on diverse themes, speeches that the eloquent and dialogues that philosophers have praised. Nay, and I write all these and much besides with equal fluency in Greek and Latin, with equal pleasure, like ardour and uniform skill. Most excellent proconsul, I would I could offer all these works of mine not in fragments and quotations but in entirety and completeness! Would I might enjoy the priceless boon of your testimony to the merits of all the offspring of my muse! It is not that I lack praise, for my glory has long bloomed fresh and bright before the eyes of all your predecessors, till to-day it is presented to you! But there is none whose admiration I would more gladly win than yours, for I admire you beyond all other men by reason of your surpassing virtues. Such is the ordinance of nature. Praise implies love and, love once given to another, we demand his praise in return. And I acknowledge that I love you; no private tie of interest binds me to you, it is in your public capacity that you have won my devotion. I have never received any favour at your hands, for I have never asked for one. But philosophy has taught me not only to love my benefactors, but even such as may have done me injury, to attach greater importance to justice than to my private interests, and to prefer the furtherance of the public welfare to the service of my own. And so it comes about that while most men love you for the actual benefits conferred upon them by your goodness, I love you for the zeal with which that goodness is inspired. And the secret of my devotion is this. I have seen your moderation in dealing with the affairs of the inhabitants of this province, a moderation which has won the affection of those who have come into contact with you by the benefits you have conferred on them, of those with whom you have never come into contact by the good example you have set. For while many have received your benefits, all have profited by your example. Who would not gladly learn from you by what moderation one may acquire your pleasing gravity, your severity tempered with mercy, your unruffled resolution and the kindly energy of your character? Africa has within my knowledge had no proconsul whom she reverenced more or feared less. Your year of office stands alone; for in it shame rather than fear has been the motive to set a check on crime. No other invested with your power has more often blessed, more rarely terrified: no governor has ever brought a son with him more like his father's virtues than is yours; and for this reason no proconsul has ever resided longer at Carthage than have you. For during the period which you devoted to visiting the province, Honorinus remained with us; wherefore, though we have never regretted our governor's absence more, we have felt it less. For the son has all his father's sense of justice, the youth has all an old man's wisdom, the deputy has all the consul's authority. In a word, he presents such a perfect pattern and likeness of your virtues, that the glory acquired by one so young would, I vow, be a greater source of wonder than your own, save for one fact; he has inherited it from you. Would we might live in the joy of his perpetual presence! What need have we of change of governors? What profit of these short years, these fleeting months of office? Ah! how swiftly pass the days, when the good are with us, how quickly spent the term of power for all the best of those who have ruled over us! Ah! Severianus, the whole province will sigh for your departure. But Honorinus at least is called away by the honours which are his due; the praetorship awaits him; the favour of the two Caesars forms him for the consulate; to-day our love enfolds him, and the hopes of Carthage promise that in the years to come he will be here once more. Your example is our sole comfort; he who has served as deputy shall soon return to us as proconsul!

On Providence and its marvels.

10. *First hail we thee, <u>O Sun</u>,*
Whose fiery course and rushing steeds reveal
The glowing splendour of thy ardent flame.

Hail we also the Moon, who learns of his light how she herself may shine, and the influences also of the five planets—Jupiter that brings blessings, Venus that brings pleasure, <u>Mercury</u> the giver of swiftness, Saturn the worker of bane, Mars with his temper of fire. There are also <u>other divine influences, that lie midway</u> 'twixt earth and heaven, influences that we may feel but not see, such as the power of Love and the like, whose force we feel, though we have never seen their form. So too on earth 'tis this force that, in accordance with the wise behests of providence, here bids the lofty peaks of mountains rise, there has spread forth the low flat levels of the plain, has marked out the streams of rivers and the greensward of the meadows, has given birds the power to fly, reptiles to crawl, wild beasts to run, and men to walk.

A comparison between those who lack wealth and those who lack virtue.

11. He whose soul is barren of virtue is like those poor wretches that till a barren inheritance of stony fields, mere heaps of rocks and thorns. Since they may win no harvest from their own wildernesses, and find no fruit in a soil where only

Wild oats and <u>darnel</u> rank have mastery,

conscious of their own poverty they go forth to steal the fruits of others and rifle their gardens, that they may mingle their neighbours' flowers with their own thistles.

On the Parrot.

12. The parrot is an Indian bird, in size very slightly smaller than a dove. But there is nothing dovelike in its hue. For it has nothing of the milky whiteness or dull blue, blended or distinct, nor yet of the pale yellow or iridescence that characterize the dove. The parrot is green from the roots of its feathers to their very tips, save only for the markings on the neck. For its tiny neck is girdled and crowned with a slender band of crimson like a collar of gold, which is of equal brilliance through all its extent. Its beak is extraordinarily hard. If after it has soared to a great height it swoops headlong on to some rock, it breaks the force of its fall with its beak, which it uses as an anchor. Its head is not less hard than its beak. When it is being taught to imitate human speech, it is beaten over the head with an iron wand, that it may recognize its master's command. This is the rod of its school-days. It can be taught to speak from the day of its birth to its second year, while its mouth

is still easily formed and its tongue sufficiently soft to learn the requisite modulations. On the other hand, if caught when it is old, it is hard to teach and forgets what it has learned. The parrot which is most easily taught the language of man is one that feeds on acorns and manlike has five toes on each foot. All parrots do not possess this last peculiarity, but there is one point which all have in common: their tongue is broader than that of any other bird. Wherefore they articulate human words more easily owing to the size of their palate and the organ of speech. When it has learnt anything, it sings or rather speaks it out with such perfect imitation that, if you should hear it, you would think a man was speaking; on the contrary if you hear a crow[42] attempting to speak, you would still call the result croaking rather than speech. But crow and parrot are alike in this; they can only utter words that they have been taught. Teach a parrot to curse and it will curse continually, making night and day hideous with its imprecations. Cursing becomes its natural note and its ideal of melody. When it has repeated all its curses, it repeats the same strain again. Should you desire to rid yourself of its bad language, you must either cut out its tongue or send it back as soon as possible to its native woods.

A comparison between the eloquence of the philosopher and the song of birds.

13. ... For the eloquence bestowed on me by philosophy has no resemblance to the song that nature has given to certain birds which sing but for a brief space and at certain times only. For instance, the swallows sing at morn, the cicalas at noon, the night-owl late in the dark, the screech-owl at even, the horned-owl at midnight, the cock before the dawn. Indeed these animals seem to have made a compact together as to the various times and tones of their song. The crowing of the cock is a sound should wake men from their beds, the horned-owl groans, the screech-owl shrieks, the night-owl cries 'tuwhit, tuwhoo', the cicalas chatter, and the swallows twitter shrill. But the wisdom and eloquence of the philosopher are ready at all times, waken awe in them that hear, are profitable to the understanding, and their music is of every tone.

On Crates the Cynic.

14. These arguments and the like which he had heard from the lips of Diogenes, together with others which suggested themselves to him on other occasions, had such influence with Crates, that at last he rushed out into the market-place and there renounced all his fortune as being a mere filthy encumbrance, a burden rather than a benefit. His action having caused a crowd to collect, he cried in a loud voice, saying, 'Crates, even Crates sets thee free.' Thenceforth he lived not only in solitude, but naked and in perfect freedom and, so long as he lived, his life was happy. And such was the

passion he inspired that a maiden of noble birth, spurning suitors more youthful and more wealthy than he, actually went so far as to beg him to marry her. In answer Crates bared his shoulders which were crowned with a hump, placed his wallet, staff and cloak upon the ground, and said to the girl, 'There is all my gear! and your eyes can judge of my beauty. Take good counsel, lest later I find you complaining of your lot.' But Hipparche accepted his conditions, replying that she had already considered the question and taken sufficient counsel, for nowhere in all the world could she find a richer or a fairer husband. 'Take me where you will!' she cried....

Of the isle of Samos and Pythagoras.

15. Samos is an island of no great size in the Icarian sea, and lies over against Miletus to the west, with but a small space of sea between them. In whichever direction you sail from this island, though you make no great haste, the next day will see you safe in harbour. The land does not respond readily to the cultivation of corn, and it is waste of time to plough it. But the olive grows better in it, and those who grow vines or vegetables have no fault to find with it. Its farmers are entirely taken up with hoeing the ground and the cultivation of trees, for it is from these rather than from cereals that Samos derives its wealth. The native population is numerous, and the island is visited by many strangers. The capital town is unworthy of its reputation, but the abundant ruins of its walls testify to its former size.

It possesses, however, a temple of Juno famous from remote antiquity: to reach it, if I remember aright, one must follow the shore for not more than twenty furlongs from the city. The treasury of the goddess is extraordinarily rich, containing great quantities of gold and silver plate, in the form of platters, mirrors, cups, and all manner of utensils. There is also a great quantity of brazen images of different kinds. These are of great antiquity, and remarkable for their workmanship; I may mention one of them in particular, a statue of Bathyllus standing in front of the altar; it was the gift of the tyrant Polycrates, and I think I have never seen anything more perfect. Some hold that it represents Pythagoras, but this opinion is incorrect. The statue represents a youth of remarkable beauty; his hair is parted evenly in the midst of his forehead and streams over either cheek. Behind his hair is longer and reaches down to his shoulders, covering the neck whose sheen one may detect between the tresses. The neck is plump, the jaws full, the cheeks fine, and there is a dimple in the middle of his chin. His pose is that of a player on the lyre. He is looking at the goddess, and has the appearance of one that sings, while his embroidered tunic streams to his very feet. He is girt in the Greek style, and a cloak covers either arm down to the wrists. The rest of the cloak hangs down in graceful folds. His lyre is fastened by an engraven baldric, which holds it close to the body. His hands are delicate and taper. The left touches the strings with parted fingers, the right is in the attitude of one that plays and is approaching the lyre with the plectrum, as though ready to strike as soon as the voice ceases for a moment to sing. Meanwhile the song seems to well forth from the delicate mouth, whose lips are half open for the effort. This statue may represent one of the youthful favourites of the tyrant Polycrates[43] hymning his master's love in Anacreontic[44] strain. But it is far from[45] likely that it is a statue of the philosopher Pythagoras. It is true he was a native of Samos, remarkable for his unusual beauty, and skilled beyond all men in harping and all manner of music, and living at the period when Polycrates was lord of Samos. But the philosopher was far from being a favourite of this tyrant. Indeed Pythagoras fled secretly from the island at the very beginning of the tyrant's reign. He had recently lost his father Mnesarchus, who was, I read, a skilful jeweller excelling in the carving of gems, though it was fame rather than wealth that he sought in the exercise of his art. There are some who assert that Pythagoras was about this time carried to Egypt among the captives of King Cambyses, and studied under the *magi* of Persia, more especially under Zoroaster the priest of all holy mysteries; later they assert he was ransomed by a certain Gillus, King of Croton. However, the more generally accepted tradition asserts that it was of his own choice he went to study the wisdom of the Egyptians. There he was initiated by their priests into the mighty secrets of their ceremonies, passing all belief; there he learned numbers in all their marvellous combinations, and the ingenious laws of geometry. Not content with these sciences, he next approached the Chaldaeans and the Brahmins, a race of wise men who live in India.[46] Among these Brahmins he sought out the gymnosophists. The Chaldaeans taught him the lore of the stars, the fixed orbits[47] of the wandering lords of heaven, and the influence of each on the births of men. Also they instructed him in the art of healing, and revealed to him remedies in the search for which men have lavished their wealth and wandered far by land and sea.[48] But it was from the Brahmins that he derived the greater part of his philosophy, the arts of teaching the mind and exercising the body, the doctrines as to the parts of the soul and its various transmigrations, the knowledge of the torments and rewards ordained for each man, according to his deserts, in the world of the gods below. Further he had for his master <u>Pherecydes</u>, a native of the island of Syros and the first who dared throw off the shackles of verse and write in the free style of unfettered prose. Pherecydes died of a horrible disease, for his flesh rotted and was devoured of lice; Pythagoras buried him with reverent care He is said also to have studied the laws of nature under <u>Anaximander</u> of Miletus, to have followed the Cretan <u>Epimenides</u>, a famous prophet skilled also in rites of expiation, that he might learn from him and also <u>Leodamas</u>, the pupil of <u>Creophylus</u>, the reputed guest and rival of the poet Homer. Taught by so many sages, and having drained such deep and varied draughts of learning through all the world, and being moreover dowered with a vast intellect whose grandeur almost passes man's understanding, he was the founder of the science and the inventor of the name of philosophy. The first of all his lessons to his disciples was the lesson of silence. With him meditation was a necessary preliminary to wisdom, meditation set a bridle on all speech, robbed words, which poets style winged, of their pinions and restrained them within the white barrier of the teeth. This, I tell you, was for him the first axiom of wisdom, 'Meditation is learning, speech is unlearning.' His disciples, however, did not refrain from speech all their lives, nor did their master impose dumbness on all for a like space of time. For those of more solid character a brief term of silence was considered sufficient discipline; the more talkative were punished by exile from speech for as much as five years. I may add that my master Plato deviates little or not at all from the principles of this school, and in most of his utterances is a follower of Pythagoras. And that I too might win from my instructors the right to be called one of his followers, I have learned this double lesson in the course of my philosophical studies—to speak boldly when there is need of speech and gladly to be mute when there is need of silence. As a result of this self-command, I think I may say that I have won from your predecessors no less praise for my seasonable silence than approval for the timeliness of my speech.

An oration of thanks to Aemilianus Strabo and the senate of Carthage for decreeing a statue in his honour.

16. Before I begin, illustrious representatives of Africa, to thank you for the statue, with the demand for which you honoured me while I was still with you, setting the seal upon your kindness by actually decreeing its erection during my absence, I wish first to explain to you why I absented myself for a considerable number of days from the sight of my audience and betook myself to the Persian baths, where the healthy may find delightful bathing, and the sick a no less welcome relief. For I have resolved to make it clear to you, to whose service I have dedicated myself irrevocably and for ever, that every moment of my life is well spent. There shall be no action of mine, important or trivial, but you shall be informed of it and pass judgement upon it. Well then! to come to the reason for my sudden departure from the presence of this most distinguished assembly, I will tell you a story of the comic poet Philemon which is not so very unlike my own and will serve to show you how sudden and unexpected are the perils that threaten the life of man. You all are well acquainted with his talents, listen then to a few words concerning his death, or perhaps you would like a few words on his talents as well.

This Philemon was a poet, a writer of the middle comedy, and composed plays for the stage in competition with Menander and contested against him. He may not have been his equal, he was certainly his rival. Nay, on not a few occasions—I am almost ashamed to mention it—he actually defeated him.

However this may be, you will certainly find his works full of humour: the plots are full of wittily contrived intrigue, the *dénouements* clear, the characters suited to the situations, the words true to life, the jests never unworthy of true comedy, the serious passages never quite on the level of tragedy. Seductions are rare in his plays; if he introduces love affairs, it is as a concession to human weakness. That does not, however, prevent the presence in his plays of the faithless pander, the passionate lover, the cunning slave, the coquetting mistress, the jealous wife whose word is law, the indulgent mother, the crusty uncle, the friend in need, the warlike soldier, aye and hungry parasites, skinflint parents, and saucy drabs. One day, long after these excellences had made him famous as a writer of comedy, he happened to give a recitation of a portion of a play which he had just written. He had reached the third act, and was beginning to arouse in his audience those pleasurable emotions so dear to comedy, when a sudden shower descended and forced him to put off the audience gathered to hear him and the recitation which he had just begun. A similar event befell me, you will remember, quite recently when I was addressing you. However, Philemon, at the demand of various persons, promised to finish his recitation the next day without further postponement. On the morrow, therefore, a vast crowd assembled to hear him with the utmost enthusiasm. Everybody who could do so took a seat facing the stage and as near to it as he could get. Late arrivals made signs to their friends to make room for them to sit: those who sat at the end of a row complained of being thrust off their seat into the gangway; the whole theatre was crammed with a vast audience. A hum of conversation[49] arose. Those who had not been present the previous day began to ask what had been recited; those who had been present began to recall what they had heard, and finally when everybody had made themselves acquainted with what had preceded, all began to look forward to what was to come. Meanwhile the day wore on and Philemon failed to come at the appointed time. Some blamed the poet for the delay, more defended him. But when they had sat there for quite an unreasonable length of time and still Philemon did not make his appearance, some of the more active members of the audience were sent to fetch him. They found him lying in his bed—dead. He had just breathed his last, and lay there upon the couch stiff and stark in the attitude of one plunged in meditation. His fingers still were twined about his book, his mouth still pressed against the page he had been reading. But the life had left him; he had forgotten his book, and little recked he now of his audience. Those who had entered the room stood motionless for a space, struck dumb by the strange suddenness of the blow and the wondrous beauty of his death. Then they returned and reported to the people that the poet Philemon, for whom they were waiting that there in the theatre he might finish the drama of his imagination, had finished the one true play, the drama of life, in his own home. To this world he had said 'farewell' and 'applaud', but to his friends 'weep and make your moan'. 'The shower of yesterday,' they continued, 'was an omen of our tears; the comedy has ended in the torch of funeral or ever it could come to the torch of marriage. Nay, since so great a poet has laid aside the mask of this life, let us go straight from the theatre to perform his burial. 'Tis his bones we now must gather to our hearts; his verse must for awhile take second place.'

It was long ago that I first learned the story I have just told you, but the peril I have undergone during the last few days[50] has brought it afresh to my mind. For when my recitation was—as I am sure you remember—interrupted by the rain, at your desire I put it off till the morrow, and in good truth it was nearly with me as it was with Philemon. For on that same day I twisted my ankle so violently at the wrestling school that I almost tore the joint from my leg. However, it returned to its socket, though my leg is still weak with the sprain. But there is more to tell you. My efforts to reduce the dislocation were so great that my body broke out into a profuse sweat and I caught a severe chill. This was followed by agonizing pain in my bowels, which only subsided when its violence was on the point of killing me. A moment more and like Philemon I should have gone to the grave, not to my recital, should have finished not my speech but my destiny, should have brought not my tale but my life to a close. Well then, as soon as the gentle temperature and still more the soothing medical properties of the Persian baths had restored to me the use of my foot—for though it gave naught save the most feeble support, it sufficed me in my eagerness to appear before you—I set forth to perform my pledge. And in the interval you have conferred such a boon upon me that you have not only removed my lameness but have made me positively nimble.

Was I not right to make all speed that I might express my boundless gratitude for the honour which you have conferred unasked. True, Carthage is so illustrious a city that it were an honour to her that a philosopher should beg to be thus rewarded, but I wished the boon you have bestowed on me to have its full value with no taint of detraction, to suffer no loss of grace by any petition on my part, in a word to be wholly disinterested. For he that begs pays so heavily, and so large is the price that he to whom the petition is addressed receives, that, where the necessaries of life are concerned, one had rather purchase them one and all than ask them as a gift. Above all, this principle applies to cases where honours are concerned. He to whom they come as the result of importunate petition owes[51] no gratitude for his success to any save himself. On the other hand, he who receives honours without descending to vexatious canvassing is obliged to the givers for two reasons; he has not asked and yet he has received. The thanks, therefore, which I owe you are double or rather manifold, and my lips shall proclaim them at all times and places. But on the present occasion I will, as is my wont, make public protestation of my gratitude from a written address which I have specially composed in view of this distinction. For assuredly that is the method in which a philosopher should return thanks to a city that has decreed him a public statue. My discourse will, however, depart slightly from this method as a mark of respect to the exalted character and position of Aemilianus Strabo. I hope that I may be able to compose a suitable discourse if only you will permit me to submit it to your approbation[52] to-day. For Strabo is so distinguished a scholar, that his own talents bring him even greater honour than his noble rank and his tenure of the consulate. In what terms, Aemilianus Strabo, who of all men that have been, are, or yet shall be, are most renowned among the virtuous, most virtuous among the renowned, most learned amongst either, in what terms can I hope to thank or commemorate the gracious thoughts you have entertained for me? How may I hope adequately to celebrate the honour to which your kindness has prompted you? How may my speech repay you worthily for the glory conferred by your action? It baffles my imagination. But I will seek earnestly and strive to find a way

*While breath still rules these limbs and memory
Is conscious of its being.*

For at the present moment, I will not deny it, the gladness of my heart is too loud for my eloquence, I cannot think for pleasure, delight is master of my soul and bids me rejoice rather than speak. What shall I do? I wish to show my gratitude, but my joy is such that I have not yet leisure to express my thanks. No one, however sour and stern he be, will blame me if the honour bestowed on me makes me no less nervous[53] than appreciative, if the testimony to my merits, delivered by a man of such fame and learning, has transported me with exultation. For he delivered it in the senate of Carthage, a body whose kindness is only equalled by its distinction; and he that spoke was one who had held the consulship, one by whom it were an honour even to be known. Such was the man who appeared before the most illustrious citizens of the province of Africa to sing my praise!

I have been told that two days ago he sent a written request in which he demanded that my statue should be given a conspicuous place, and above all told of the bonds of friendship which began under such honourable circumstances, when we served together beneath the banner of literature and studied under the same masters; he then recorded[54] all the good wishes for his success with which I had welcomed each successive step of his advance in his official career. He had already done me a compliment in remembering that I had once been his fellow student: it was a fresh compliment that so great a man should record my friendship for him as though I were his equal. But he went further. He stated that other peoples and cities had decreed not only statues, but other distinctions as well in my honour. Could anything be added to such a panegyric as this, delivered by the lips of an ex-consul? Yes: for he cited the priesthood I had undertaken, and showed that I had attained the highest honour that Carthage can bestow. But the greatest and most remarkable compliment[55] paid me was this: after producing such a wealth of flattering testimonials he commended me to your notice by himself voting in my favour. Finally, he, a man in whose honour every province rejoices through all the world to erect four or six horse chariots, promised that he would erect my statue at Carthage at his own expense.

What lacks there to sanction and establish my glory and to set it on the topmost pinnacle of fame? I ask you, what is there lacking? Aemilianus Strabo, who has already held the consulship and is destined, as we all hope and pray, soon to be a proconsul, proposed the resolution conferring these honours upon me in the senate-house of Carthage. You gave your unanimous assent to the proposal. Surely in your eyes this was more than a mere resolution, it was a solemn enactment of law. Nay more, all the Carthaginians gathered in this august assembly showed such readiness in granting a site for the statue that they might make it clear to you that, if they put off a resolution for the erection of a second statue, as I hope,[56] to the next meeting of the senate, they were influenced by the desire to show the fullest reverence and respect to their honourable consular, and to avoid seeming to emulate rather than imitate his beneficence. That is to say, they wished to set apart a whole day for the business of conferring on me the public honour still in store. Moreover, these most excellent magistrates, these most gracious chiefs of your city, remembered that the charge with which you men of Carthage had entrusted them was in full harmony with their desires. Would you have me be ignorant, be silent, as to these details? It would be rank ingratitude. Far from that, I offer my very warmest thanks to the whole assembly for their most lavish favour. I could not be more grateful. For they have honoured me with the most flattering applause in that senate-house, where even to be named is the height of honour. And so I have in some sense achieved—pardon my vanity—that which was so hard to achieve, and seemed indeed not unnaturally to be beyond my powers. I have won the affections of the people, the favour of the senate, the approbation of the magistrates and the chief men of the city. What lacks there now to the honour of my statue, save the price of the bronze and the service of the artist? These have never been denied me even in small cities. Much less shall Carthage deny it, Carthage, whose senate, even where greater issues are at stake, decrees and counts not the cost. But I will speak of this more fully at a later date, when you have given fuller effect to your resolution. Moreover, when the time comes for the dedication of my statue, I will proclaim my gratitude to you yet more amply in another written discourse, will declare it to you, noble senators, to you, renowned citizens, to you, my worthy friends. Yes, I will commit my gratitude to the retentive pages of a book, that it may travel through every province and, worlds and ages hence, record my praises of your kindness to all peoples and all time.

Fragment of a panegyric on Scipio Orfitus.

17. I leave it to those who are in the habit of obtruding themselves upon their proconsul's leisure moments[57] to attempt to commend their wits by the exuberance of their speech, and to glorify themselves by affecting to bask in the smiles of your friendship. Both of these offences are far from me, Scipio Orfitus. For on the one hand my poor wit, such as it is, is too well known to all men to have any need of further commendation; on the other hand, I prefer to enjoy rather than to parade the friendship of yourself and such as you; I desire such friendship, but I do not boast of it, for desire can in no case be other than genuine, whereas boasting may always be false. With this in view I have ever cultivated the arts of virtue, I have always sought both here in Africa and when I moved among your friends in Rome to win a fair name both for my character and studies, as you yourself can amply testify, with the result that you should be no less eager to court my friendship than I to long for yours. Reluctance to excuse the rarity of a friend's appearances is a sign that you desire his continual presence; if you delight in the frequency of his visits or are angry with him for neglecting to come, if you welcome his company and regret its cessation, it is clear proof of love, since it is obvious that his presence must be a pleasure whose absence is a pain. But the voice, if it be refrained in continued silence, is as useless as the nostrils when choked by a cold in the head, the ears when they are blocked with dirt, the eyes when they are sealed by cataract. What can the hands do, if they are fettered, or what the feet, if they are shackled? What can[58] the mind that rules and directs us do, if it be relaxed in sleep or drowned in wine or crushed beneath the weight of disease? Nay, as the sword acquires its sheen by usage, and rusts if it lie idle, so the voice is dulled by its long torpor if it be hidden in the sheath of silence. Desuetude must needs beget sloth, and sloth decay. If the tragic actor declaim not daily, the resonance of his voice is dulled and its channels grow hoarse. Wherefore he purges his huskiness by loud and repeated recitation. However, it is vain toil and useless labour[59] for a man to attempt to improve the natural quality of the human voice. There are many sounds that surpass it. The trumpet's blare is louder, the music of the lyre more varied, the plaint of the flute more pleasing, the murmurs of the pipe sweeter, the message of the bugle further heard. I forbear to mention the natural sounds of many animals which challenge admiration by their different peculiarities, as, for instance, the deep bellow

of the bull, the wolf's shrill howl, the dismal trumpeting of the elephant, the horse's lively neigh, the bird's piercing song, the angry roar of the lion, together with the cries of other beasts, harsh or musical, according as they are roused by the madness of anger or the charms of pleasure. In place of such cries the gods have given man a voice of narrower compass; but if it give less delight to the ear, it is far more useful to the understanding. Wherefore it should be all the more cultivated by the most frequent use, and that nowhere else[60] than in the presence of an audience presided over by so great a man, and in the midst of so numerous and distinguished a gathering of learned men who come kindly disposed to hear. For my part, if I were skilled to make ravishing music on the lyre, I should never play save before crowded assemblies. It was in solitude that

<u>Orpheus to woods</u>, to fish Arion sang.

For if we may believe legend, Orpheus had been driven to lonely exile, Arion hurled from his ship. One of them soothed savage beasts, the other charmed beasts that were compassionate: both musicians were unhappy, inasmuch as they strove not for honour nor of their free choice, but for their safety and of hard necessity. I should have admired them more if they had pleased men, not beasts. Such solitude were far better suited to birds, to blackbird and nightingale and swan. The blackbird whistles like a happy boy in distant wilds, the nightingale trills its song of youthful passion in the lonely places of Africa, the swan by far-off rivers chants the music of old age. But he who would produce a song that shall profit boys, youths, and greybeards, must sing it in the midst of thousands of men, even as now I sing the virtues of Orfitus. It is late, perhaps, but it is meant in all earnestness, and may prove no less pleasing than profitable to the boys, the youths, and the old men of Carthage. For all have enjoyed the indulgence of the best of all proconsuls: he has tempered their desires and restrained them with gentle remedies, he has given to boys the boon of plenty, to young men merriment, and to the old security. But now, Scipio, that I have come to touch on your merits, I fear lest either your own noble modesty or my own native bashfulness may close my mouth. But I cannot refrain from touching on a very few of the many virtues which we so justly admire in you. Citizens whom he has saved, show with me that you recognize them!

A discourse pronounced before the Carthaginians, incidentally treating of Thales and Protagoras.

18. You have come in such large numbers to hear me that I feel I ought rather to congratulate Carthage for possessing so many friends of learning among her citizens than demand pardon for myself, the professed philosopher who ventures to speak in public. For the crowd that has collected is worthy of the grandeur of our city, and the place chosen for my

speech is worthy of so great a multitude. Moreover, in a theatre we must consider, not the marble of its pavements, not the boards of the stage, nor the columns of the back-scene, nay, nor yet the height of its gables, the splendour of its fretted roofs, the expanse of its tiers of seats; we need not call to mind that this place is sometimes the scene for the foolery of the mime, the dialogue of comedy, the sonorous rant of tragedy, the perilous antics of the rope-walker, the juggler's sleight of hand, the gesticulation of the dancer, with all the tricks of their respective arts that are displayed before the people by other artists. All these considerations may be put on one side; all that we need consider is this, the discourse of the orator and the reasons for the presence of the audience. Wherefore, just as poets in this place shift the scene to various other cities—take, for instance, the tragic poet who makes his actor say

Liber, that dwellest on these heights august
Of famed Cithaeron

or the comic poet who says

Plautus but asks you for a tiny space
Within the circuit vast of these fair walls,
Whither without the aid of architect
He may transport old Athens,—

even so I beg your leave to shift my scene, not, however, to any distant city overseas, but to the senate-house or public library of Carthage. I ask you, therefore, if any of my utterances be worthy of the senate-house, to imagine that you are listening to me within the very walls of the senate-house; if my words reveal learning, I beg you to regard them as though you were reading them in the public library. Would that I could find words enough to do justice to the magnitude of this assembly and did not falter just when I would be most eloquent. But the old saying is true, that heaven never blesses any man with unmixed and flawless prosperity; even in the keenest joys there is ever some slight undertone of grief, some blend of gall and honey; there is no rose without a thorn. I have often experienced the truth of this, and never more than at the present moment. For the more I realize how ready you are to praise me, the more exaggerated becomes the awe in which I stand of you, and the greater my reluctance to speak. I have spoken to strange audiences often, and with the utmost fluency, but now that I am confronted with my own folk, I hesitate. Strange to say, I am frightened by what should allure, curbed by what should spur me on, and restrained by what should make me bold. There is much that should give me courage in your presence. I have made my home in your city which I knew well as a boy, and where my student days were spent. You know my philosophic views, my voice is no stranger to you, you have read my books and approved of them. My birthplace is represented in the council of Africa, that is, in your own assembly; my boyhood was spent with you, you were my teachers, it was here that my philosophy found its first inspiration, though 'twas Attic Athens brought it to maturity, and, during the last six years, my voice, speaking in either language, has been familiar to your ears. Nay more, my books have no higher title to the universal praise that is theirs, than the fact that you have passed a favourable judgement upon them. All these great and varied allurements, appealing as they do to you as well as to me, hamper and intimidate me just in proportion as they attract you to the pleasure of hearing me. I should find it far easier to sing your praises before the citizens of some other city than to your face. To such an extent is it true that modesty is a serious obstacle to one confronted by his fellow citizens, while truth may speak unfettered in the presence of strangers. But always and everywhere I praise you as my parents and the first teachers of my youth, and do my best to repay my debt. But the reward I offer you is not that which the sophist Protagoras stipulated to receive and never got, but that which the wise Thales got without ever stipulating for it. What is it you want? Ah! I understand. I will tell you both stories.

Protagoras was a sophist with knowledge on an extraordinary number of subjects, and one of the most eloquent among the first inventors of the art of rhetoric. He was a fellow citizen and contemporary of the physicist Democritus, and it was from Democritus he derived his learning. The story runs that Protagoras made a rash bargain with his pupil Euathlus, contracting for an exceptionally high fee on the following conditions. The money was to be paid if Euathlus was successful in the first suit he pleaded in court. The young man therefore first learned all the methods employed to win the votes of the jurors, all the tricks of opposing counsel, and all the artifices of oratory. This he did with ease, for he was a very clever fellow with a natural aptitude for strategy. When he had satisfied himself that he had learned all he desired to know, he began to show reluctance to perform his part of the contract. At first he baffled his teacher's requests for payment by interposing various ingenious delays, and for a considerable time refused either to plead in court or to pay the stipulated fee. At last Protagoras called him into court, set forth the conditions under which he had accepted him as a pupil, and propounded the following dilemma. 'If I win,' he said, 'you must pay the fee, for you will be condemned to do so. If you win, you will still have to pay under the terms of your contract. For you will have won the first suit you have ever pleaded. So if you win, you lose under the terms of the contract: if you are defeated, you lose by the sentence of the court.' What more would you have? The jury thought the argument a marvel of shrewdness and quite irrefutable. But Euathlus showed himself a very perfect pupil of so cunning a master, and turned back the dilemma on its inventor. 'In that case,' he replied, 'I owe your fee under neither count. For either I win and am acquitted by the court, or lose and am released from the bargain, which states that I do not owe you the fee if I am defeated in my first case in court. And this is my first case! So in any case I come off scot free; if I lose, I am saved by the contract; if I win, by the verdict of the jury.' What think you? Does not the opposition of these sophistic arguments remind you of brambles, that the wind has entangled one with another? They cling together; thorns of like length on either side, each penetrating to an equal depth, each dealing wound for wound. So we will leave Protagoras' reward to shrewd and greedy folk. It involves too many thorny difficulties. Far better is that other reward, which they say was suggested by[61] Thales.

Thales of Miletus was easily the most remarkable of the famous seven sages. For he was the first of the Greeks to discover the science of geometry, was a most accurate investigator of the laws of nature, and a most skilful observer of the stars. With the help of a few small lines he discovered the most momentous facts: the revolution of the years, the blasts of the winds, the wanderings of the stars, the echoing miracle of thunder, the slanting path of the zodiac, the annual turnings of the sun, the waxing of the moon when young, her waning when she has waxed old, and the shadow of her eclipse; of all these he discovered the laws. Even when he was far advanced into the vale of years, he evolved a divinely inspired theory concerning the period of the sun's revolution through the circle in which he moves in all his majesty. This theory, I may say, I have not only learned from books, but have also proved its truth by experiment. This theory Thales is said to have taught soon after its discovery to Mandraytus of Priene. The latter, fascinated by the strangeness and novelty of his newly acquired knowledge, bade Thales choose whatever recompense he might desire in return for such precious instruction. 'It is enough recompense,' replied Thales the wise, 'if you will refrain from claiming as your own the theory I have taught you, whenever you begin to impart it to others, and will proclaim me and no other as the discoverer of this new law.' In truth that was a noble recompense, worthy of so great a man and beyond the reach of time. For that recompense has been paid to Thales down to this very day, and shall be paid to all eternity by all of us who have realized the truth of his discoveries concerning the heavens.

Such is the recompense I pay you, citizens of Carthage, through all the world, in return for the instruction that Carthage gave me as a boy. Everywhere I boast myself your city's nursling, everywhere and in every way I sing your praises, do zealous honour to your learning, give glory to your wealth and reverent worship to your gods. Now, therefore, I will begin by speaking of the god Aesculapius. With what more auspicious theme could I engage your ears? For he honours the citadel of our own Carthage with the protection of his undoubted presence. See, I will sing to you both in Greek and Latin a hymn which I have composed to his glory and long since dedicated to him. For I am well known as a frequenter of his rites, my worship of him is no new thing, my priesthood has received the smile of his favour, and ere now I have expressed my veneration for him both in prose and verse. Even so now I will chant a hymn to his glory both in Greek and Latin. I have prefaced it with a dialogue likewise in both tongues, in which Sabidius Severus and Julius Persius shall speak together. They are men who are deservedly bound alike to one another, and to you and the public weal by the closest ties of friendship. Both are equally distinguished for their learning, their eloquence, and their benevolence. It is difficult to say whether they are more remarkable for their great moderation, their ready energy, or the distinction of their career. They are united one to another by the most complete harmony. There is but one point on which rivalry exists between them, namely this: they dispute which has the greater love for Carthage; for this they contend with all their strength and all their soul, and neither is vanquished in the contest. Thinking, then, that you would be most delighted to listen to their converse, and that such a theme suited my powers and would be a welcome offering to the god, I begin at the outset of my book by making one of my fellow students of Athens demand of Persius in Greek what was the subject of the declamation delivered by myself on the previous day in the temple of Aesculapius. As the dialogue proceeds I introduce Severus to their company. His part is written in the language of Rome. For Persius, although a master of Latin, shall yet to-day speak to you in the Attic tongue.

A story of the physician Asclepiades.

19. The famous Asclepiades, who ranks among the greatest of doctors, indeed, if you except Hippocrates, as the very greatest, was the first to discover the use of wine as a remedy. It requires, however, to be administered at the proper moment, and it was in the discovery of the right moment that he showed especial skill, noting most carefully the slightest symptom of disorder or undue rapidity of the pulse. It chanced that once, when he was returning to town from his country house, he observed an enormous funeral procession in the suburbs of the city. A huge multitude of men who had come out to perform the last honours stood round about the bier, all of them plunged in deep sorrow and wearing worn and ragged apparel. He asked whom they were burying, but no one replied; so he went nearer[62] to satisfy his curiosity and to see who it might be that was dead, or, it may be, in the hope to make some discovery in the interests of his profession. Be this as it may, he certainly snatched the man from the jaws of death as he lay there on the verge of burial. The poor fellow's limbs were already covered with spices, his mouth filled with sweet-smelling unguent. He had been anointed and was all ready for the pyre. But Asclepiades looked upon him, took careful note of certain signs, handled his body again and again and perceived that the life

was still in him, though scarcely to be detected. Straightway he cried out 'He lives! Throw down your torches, take away your fire demolish the pyre, take back the funeral feast and spread it on his board at home'. While he spoke a murmur arose; some said that they must take the doctor's word, others mocked at the physician's skill. At last, in spite of the opposition offered even by his relations, perhaps because they had already entered into possession of the dead man's property, perhaps because they did not yet believe his words, Asclepiades persuaded them to put off the burial for a brief space. Having thus rescued him from the hands of the undertaker, he carried the man home, as it were from the very mouth of hell, and straightway revived the spirit within him, and by means of certain drugs called forth the life that still lay hidden in the secret places of the body.

A panegyric on his own talents.

20. There is a remarkable saying of a wise man concerning the pleasures of the table to the effect that, 'The first glass quenches thirst, the second makes merry, the third kindles desire, the fourth madness.' But in the case of a draught from the Muses' fountain the reverse is true. The more cups you drink and the more undiluted the draught the better it will be for your soul's good. The first cup is given by the master that teaches you to read and write and redeems you from ignorance[63], the second is given by the teacher of literature and equips you with learning, the third arms you with the eloquence of the rhetorician. Of these three cups most men drink. I, however, have drunk yet other cups at Athens—the imaginative draught of poetry, the clear draught of geometry, the sweet draught of music, the austerer draught of dialectic, and the nectar of all philosophy, whereof no man may ever drink enough. For Empedocles composed verse, Plato dialogues, Socrates hymns, Epicharmus music, Xenophon histories, and Xenocrates satire. But your friend Apuleius cultivates all these branches of art together and worships all nine Muses with equal zeal. His enthusiasm is, I admit, in advance of his capacity, but that perhaps makes him all the more praiseworthy, inasmuch as in all high enterprises it is the effort that merits praise, success is after all a matter of chance. As an illustration I may remind you, that the law punishes even the premeditation of crime, though the criminal's purpose may never have been carried out; the hand may be pure, but there is blood upon the soul, and that suffices. As, then, to call down the doom of law it suffices to purpose deeds meet for punishment, so to win praise it is sufficient to essay deeds worthy of the voice of fame; and what greater or surer claim to praise may any man have than to glorify Carthage? For you, her citizens, are full of learning to a man, your boys learn, your young men display, and your old men teach all manner of knowledge. Carthage is the venerable instructress of our province, Carthage is the heavenly muse of Africa, Carthage is the fount whence all the Roman world draws draughts of inspiration.

An excuse for delay caused by social duties.

21. Sometimes even when haste is most incumbent on us, the delays that slow our progress may bring such honour, that often we shall be glad to have been thwarted of our purpose. For instance, take the case of persons who are compelled to journey in such high haste, that they prefer the perils of the saddle to a seat in a carriage on account of the trouble caused by their baggage, the weight of the vehicle, the delays to progress, the roughness of the track, not to mention the boulders that beset the route, the tree trunks fallen across the way, the rivers that intersect the level, and the steep slopes of the mountains. Well, then, those who wish to avoid all these obstacles select a horse of tried endurance, mettle, and speed, that is to say, one strong to bear and swift to go, like the horse described by Lucilius that

With one sole stride o'erpasses plain and hill.

None the less, if as this horse bears them along on the wings of his speed, they chance to see some great personage, a man of noble birth, high wisdom, and universal fame, then, however pressing their haste, they refrain their speed that they may do him honour, slacken their pace and rein in their horse: then straightway leaping to the ground they transfer to their left hand the switch, which they carry wherewith to beat the horse, and with right hand thus left free approach the great man and salute him. If it please him for a while to ask questions of them, they will walk with him for a while and talk with him: in fact they will gladly suffer any amount of delay in the performance of the duty which they owe him.

On the Virtues of Crates.

22. Crates, the well-known disciple of Diogenes, was honoured at Athens by the men of his own day as though he had been a household god. No house was ever closed to him, no head of a family had ever so close a secret as to regard Crates as an unseasonable intruder: he was always welcome; there was never a quarrel, never a lawsuit between kinsfolk, but he was accepted as mediator and his word was law. The poets tell that Hercules of old by his valour subdued all the wild monsters of legend, beast or man, and purged all the world of them. Even so our philosopher was a very Hercules in the conquest of anger, envy, avarice, lust, and all the other monstrous sins that beset the human soul. He expelled all these pests from their minds, purged households, and tamed vice. Nay, he too went half-naked and was distinguished by the club he carried, aye, and he sprang from that same Thebes, where Hercules, men say, was born. Even before he became Crates pure and simple, he was accounted one of the chief men in Thebes: his family was noble, his establishment numerous, his house had a fair and ample porch: his lands were rich and his clothing sumptuous. But later, when he understood that the wealth which had been transmitted to him, carried with

it no safeguard whereon he might lean as on a staff in the ways of life, but that all was fragile and transitory, that all the wealth that is in all the world was of no assistance to a virtuous life....

On the uncertainty of fortune.

23. Imagine some good ship, wrought by skilled hands, well built within and fairly adorned without, with rudder answering to the touch, taut rigging, lofty mast, resplendent tops, and shining sails; in a word, supplied with all such gear as may serve either for use or the delight of the eye. Imagine all this and then think how easily, if the tempest and no helmsman be her guide, the deep may engulf her or the reefs grind her to pieces with all her goodly gear. Again, when physicians enter a sick man's house to visit him, none of them bids the invalid be of good cheer on account of the exquisite balconies with which they see the house to be adorned, nor on account of the fretted ceilings all overlaid with gold, or the multitudes of handsome boys and youths that stand about the couch in his chamber. Rather the physician sits down by the man's bedside, takes his hand, feels it and explores the beat and movements of the pulse. If he discovers any irregularity or disorder, he informs his patient that he is seriously ill. Our rich man is bidden fast: on that day mid all the abundant store of his own house, he touches not even bread: and meanwhile all his slaves feast and are merry, and their servile state makes no difference to them.

An improvisation.

24. You have asked me to give you an improvisation. Listen then. You have heard me speak prepared, now hear me unprepared. I think I risk but little in making an attempt to speak without premeditation in view of the extraordinary approval which I have won by my set speeches. For having pleased you by more serious efforts, I have no fear of displeasing you when I speak on a frivolous subject. But in order that you may know me in all my infinite variety, make trial of me in what Lucilius called

The improviser's formless art,

and see whether I have the same skill at short notice as I have after preparation; if indeed there be any of you who have never heard the trifles I toss off on the spur of the moment. You will listen to them with the same critical exactitude that I have bestowed on their composition, but with greater complaisance, I hope, than I can feel in reciting them. For prudent judges are wont to judge finished works by a somewhat severe standard, but are far more complaisant to improvisations. For you weigh and examine all that is actually written, but in the case of extempore speaking pardon and criticism go hand in hand, as it is right they should. For what we read forth from manuscript will remain such as it was when set down, even though you say nothing, but those words which I must utter now and the travail of whose birth you must share with me, will be just such as your favour shall make them. For the more I modify my style to suit your taste, the more I shall please you.[64] I see that you hear me gladly. From this moment it lies with you to furl or spread my sails, that they hang not slack and drooping nor be reefed and brailed.

I will try to apply the saying of Aristippus. Aristippus was the founder of the Cyrenaic school of philosophy and was a disciple of Socrates—a fact which he regarded as the greater honour of the two. A certain tyrant asked him what benefit he had derived from so long and so devoted a study of philosophy. 'It has given me the power,' replied Aristippus, 'to converse with all men without fear or concern.'

My speech has begun with a certain abruptness of expression due to the suddenness with which the subject suggested itself to me. It is as though I were building a loose wall in which one must be content to pile the stones haphazard without filling the interior with rubble, levelling the front, or making all lines true to rule. For in building up this speech I shall not bring stones from my own quarry, hewn foursquare and planed on all sides with their outer edge cut smooth and level, so that the nail slips lightly over it. No! at every point I must fit in material that is rough and uneven, or slippery and smooth, or jagged, projecting and angular, or round and rolling. There will be no correction by rule, no measure or proportion, no attention to the perpendicular. For it is impossible to produce a thing on the spur of the moment and to give it careful consideration, nor is there anything in the world that can hope at one and the same time to be praised for its care and admired for its speed.

The fable of the fox and the crow.

25. I have complied with the desire of certain persons who just now begged me to speak extempore. But, by Hercules, I fear that I may suffer the fate that befell the crow in Aesop's fable: namely, that in the attempt to win this new species of glory I may lose the little I have already acquired. What is this parable, you ask me? I will gladly turn fabulist for awhile. A crow and a fox caught sight of a morsel of food at the same moment and hurried to seize it. Their greed was equal, but their speed was not. Reynard ran, but the crow flew, with the result that the bird was too quick for the quadruped, sailed down the wind on extended pinions, outstripped and forestalled him. Then, rejoicing at his victory in the race for the booty, the crow flew into a neighbouring oak and sat out of reach on the topmost bough. The fox being unable to hurl a stone, launched a trick at him and reached him. For coming up to the foot of the tree, he stopped there, and seeing the robber high above him exulting in his booty, began to praise him with cunning words. 'Fool that

I was thus vainly to contend with Apollo's bird! For his body is exquisitely proportioned, neither exceeding small nor yet too large, but just of the size demanded by use and beauty; his plumage is soft, his head sharp and fine, his beak strong. Nay, more, he has wings with which to follow, keen eyes with which to see, and claws with which to seize his prey. As for his colour, what can I say? There are two transcendent hues, the blackness of pitch and the whiteness of snow, the colours that distinguish night and day. Both of these hues Apollo has given to the birds he loves, white to the swan and black to the crow. Would he had given the latter a voice like the sweet song he has conferred upon the swan, that so fair a bird, so far excelling all the fowls of the air, might not live, as now he lives, voiceless, the darling of the god of eloquence, but himself mute and tongueless.' When the crow heard that, though possessed of so many qualities, there yet lacked this one, he was seized with a desire to utter as loud a cry as possible, that the swan might not have the advantage of him in this respect at any rate, and forgetting the morsel which he held in his beak, he opened his mouth to its widest extent, and thus lost by his song what his wings had won him, while the fox recovered by craft what his feet had lost him. Let us reduce this fable to the smallest number of words possible. The crow, to prove himself musical—for the fox pretended that this, the absence of a voice, was the sole slur on such exquisite beauty—began to croak, and delivered over the spoil which he carried in his mouth to the enemy who had thus ensnared him.

A transition from Greek to Latin.

26. I have known for a long time what it is your demonstrations demand: namely, that I should deal with the rest of my material in Latin. For I remember that at the very beginning, when you were divided in opinion, I promised that neither party among you, neither those who insisted on Greek nor those who insisted on Latin, should go away without hearing the language he desired. Wherefore, if it seems good to you, let us consider that my speech has been Attic long enough. It is time to migrate from Greece to Latium. For we are now almost half through our inquiry and, as far as I can see, the second half does not yield to the first part which I have delivered in Greek. It is as strong in argument, as full of epigram, as rich in illustration and as admirable in style.

NOTES

THE APOLOGIA

CHAPTER 1. *Claudius Maximus*, proconsul of Africa, is spoken of as having succeeded Lollianus Avitus. Lollianus Avitus was consul in 144 A.D. As ten to thirteen years usually elapsed between tenure of the consulate and proconsulate, Lollianus Avitus may have been proconsul 154-7 A.D., and Claudius Maximus 155-8 A.D.

gentlemen who sit beside him on the bench. The governor of the province, when holding his assize, would be assisted by a *consilium* of assessors drawn partly from his staff, partly from the local *conventus civium Romanorum*.

Granii. Nothing is known of this suit. Granii are mentioned as connexions of Lollius Urbicus (C.I.L. viii. 6705).

CHAPTER 2. *Lollius Urbicus* is described a few lines lower down as *praefectus urbi*, which is borne out by an inscription (C.I.L. vi. 28). The lawsuit of Aemilianus must therefore have been heard at Rome. The explanation of the words *quam quidem vocem*, &c., which follow, imply that Lollius was now in Numidia. This is possible enough since an inscription (C.I.L. viii. 6705) proves him to have been a native of Tiddis in Numidia. The *praefectus urbi* was assisted by a *consilium*, not by *iudices*. Here the members of the *consilium* are described as *consulares*. [Cp. Karlowa, Röm. Rechtgesch., p. 551.]

CHAPTER 4. *not merely in Latin but also in Greek.* Cp. Florida, chaps. 18 and 26.

Tannonius Pudens, an advocatus of the accusers and, presumably, a relative.

Homer, sc. Il. iii. 65.

Pythagoras, inventor of the term φιλοσοφία; cp. Diog. Laert. i, proem. 12. He was a native of Samos and migrated to Croton. See Florida, chap. 15. Floruit circa 530 B.C.

Zeno of Velia or Elea in Lucania was the founder of dialectic. Floruit circa 450 B.C.

self inconsistency. The phrase *argumenta ambifariam dissolvere* is very obscure. I am indebted to Professor Cook Wilson for the following note. 'A comparison of the passage with the captious argument of Protagoras (Florida, chap. 17, *ambifariam proposuit*), which is in the form of a dilemma, might suggest that *ambifariam* in both places means "by dilemma". But this is not a natural way of describing the method of Zeno. The characteristic of his philosophy was, according to tradition, that he tried to prove the thesis of Parmenides negatively by disproving the hypothesis contradictory to it. The disproof consisted in showing that the hypothesis in question involved a contradiction. If, therefore, *ambifariam* means "by dilemma" it would appear that Apuleius did not understand the true characteristic of Zeno's method; for *dissolvere* should refer to Zeno's method of disproof, which is not properly called dilemma.

'But perhaps it is not necessary to assume such a mistake on the part of Apuleius. *Ambifariam* may mean "ambiguously" in the sense of involving both sides of a contradiction (i.e. both of two contradictory propositions). This would suit the Protagoras passage well, for the argument, as the context shows, involves a contradiction. Zeno's argumentation also could be correctly described as *ambifariam dissolvere*, because he refuted the thesis opposed to that of Parmenides by showing that it involves a contradiction. Then the meaning of the passage would be that Zeno's cleverness (*sollertissimum artificium*) lay in the use of the *reductio ad absurdum* argument. In that case the translation would be as given in the text.' I find a confirmation of Professor Cook Wilson's view in the following line, cited from Timon of Phlius by Diog. Laert. ix. v. 2, where the word ἀμφοτερόγλωσσος is used with reference to Zeno's methods of argument, sc. ἀμφοτερογλώσσου τε μέγα σθένος οὐκ ἀλαπαδνόν.

Plato, sc. Parmenides, 127*b*.

capital charge. There is an untranslatable pun here, *capitalis* bearing the double meaning 'capital' and 'pertaining to the head'.

CHAPTER 5. *Statius Caecilius*, one of the most famous writers of comedy. He died 168 B.C.

CHAPTER 6. *tooth-powder*, clearly a magical compound according to the accusers.

Catullus, sc. xxxix. 17-21.

CHAPTER 7. *the barrier of the teeth*. Homer, Odyss. i. 64.

CHAPTER 8. *the crocodile*. See Herodotus ii. 68.

CHAPTER 9. *Teian*, sc. Anacreon, circa 520 B.C.

Lacedaemonian, sc. Alcman, circa 650 B.C.

Cean, sc. Simonides, circa 520 B.C.

Lesbian, sc. Sappho, circa 600 B.C.

Aedituus, Porcius, Catulus, erotic epigrammatists of the Republican period, 130-100 B.C. The latter was Marius' colleague in the Cimbrian wars.

Solon. The line ascribed to Solon is almost too gross in the original to be genuine.

Diogenes, the founder of the Cynic school (died 324 B.C.), wrote 'concerning marriage and the begetting of children' in an erotic fashion. Diog. Laert. vi. 2. 12.

Zeno of Citium, founder of the Stoic school (died 264 B.C.), wrote an 'art of love'. Diog. Laert. vii. 21. 29.

CHAPTER 10. *Ticidas*, an erotic poet, contemporary with Catullus and, like him, belonging to the Alexandrian school.

Lucilius, the first of Rome's great satirists (148-103 B.C.), famous for the extraordinary vigour with which he lashed the vices of the age. The allusion in the present passage is unknown, though a fragment is preserved containing the name of Macedo and possibly also of Gentius (cp. Baehrens, Fragm. Poet. Rom., p. 168).

the Mantuan poet. Vergil, Ecl. ii.

Serranus, the cognomen of Atilius Regulus, consul 257 B.C., the famous Regulus of the first Punic war.

Curius Dentatus, thrice consul, and victor over the Samnites and Pyrrhus.

Fabricius, general in the war against Pyrrhus. Consul in 282 and 278 B.C. These three great soldiers were selected as types of Roman virtue. Cp. Verg. Aen. vi. 485.

Dion, brother-in-law and son-in-law of Dionysius II, tyrant of Syracuse, the friend and pupil of Plato, and for a brief space tyrant of Syracuse.

CHAPTER 11. *Catullus* xvi. 5.

Hadrian, Emperor, 117-138 A.D.

Voconius, mentioned here only.

CHAPTER 12. *Venus is not one goddess but two*. For this doctrine see Plato's Symposium, p. 181.

Afranius, the most famous writer of purely Roman comedy (*fabulae togatae*), floruit circa 110 B.C.

CHAPTER 13. *Ennius* (239-169 B.C.), the 'father of Roman Poetry'. Cp. Cic. de Or. ii. 156 'ac sic decrevi philosophari potius ut Neoptolemus apud Ennium "paucis: nam omnino haud placet"'.

the mirror, clearly regarded by the accusers, though Apuleius does not say so, as a magical instrument.

CHAPTER 15. *The Lacedaemonian Agesilaus*, the greatest of the Spartan kings, 440-360 B.C. Cp. Cic. ad Fam. v. 12.

Socrates. Cp. Diog. Laert. ii. 5, 33.

Demosthenes and *Plato.* Cp. Quint. xii. 2. 22 and 10. 23.

Eubulides, a sophist of Miletus. Cp. Diog. Laert. ii. 10. 4.

the orator when he wrangles, &c. The pun on *iurgari,* 'wrangles,' and *obiurgari,* 'rebukes,' can scarcely be reproduced. 'Disproves' and 'disapproves' would weaken the translation.

Epicurus of Samos, born 342 B.C. For his views on vision cp. Lucret. iv. 156, on mirrors, 293.

Plato. Cp. Timaeus, p. 46 A, 'Within the eyes they (the gods) planted that variety of fire which does not burn, but it is called light homogeneous with the light without. We are enabled to see in the daytime, because the light within our eyes pours out through the centre of them and commingles with the light without. The two being thus confounded together transmit movements from every object they touch through the eye inward to the soul, and thus bring about the sensation of the sight.' Grote's Plato iii. 265.

Archytas of Tarentum, a Pythagorean (circa 400 B.C.). *The Stoics*—believed that sight consisted in a refined fluid or visual effluence proceeding from the central intelligence through the eyes. 'In the process of seeing, the ὁρατικὸν πνεῦμα (visual effluence) coming into the eyes from the ἡγεμονικόν (central intelligence) gives a spherical form to the air before the eye by virtue of its τονικὴ κίνησις (i.e. the tension it sets up), and by means of the sphere of air comes in contact with things; and since by this process rays of light emanate from the eye, darkness must be visible.' Zeller, The Stoics, Epicureans, and Sceptics, p. 209, note. Cp. Plut. Plac. Phil. iv. 15.

CHAPTER 16. *two rival images of the sun.* Apparently an allusion to the phenomenon of mock suns. Archimedes had, according to Apuleius, treated of the rainbow and the mock sun in connexion with his researches into mirrors.

CHAPTER 17. *Marcus Antonius,* the orator, born 143 B.C., Consul 99 B.C.

Carbo, consul 85-82 B.C., one of the leaders of the Marian party and the chief opponent of Sulla after Marius' death.

Manius Curius. See note on chap. 10.

Marcus Cato, consul in 195 B.C., conducted a successful campaign in Spain in that and the following year.

CHAPTER 18. *Aristides,* the Athenian statesman and general, surnamed the just, died circa 468 B.C.

Phocion, an Athenian general and statesman, born 402 B.C., died 317 B.C. He was famous for his virtue and his poverty.

Epaminondas, the great Theban general who fell at Mantinea, 362 B.C. He was of noble birth but poor.

Fabricius. See note on chap. 10.

Gnaeus Scipio. Cp. Val. Max. iv. 4. 10. 'In the second Punic war Gnaeus Scipio wrote to the senate from Spain, begging that he might be replaced in his command. For his daughter was now of marriageable age, but could not be provided with a dowry during his absence from Rome.'

Publicola (*Valerius*), colleague of Brutus in the consulship in the first year of the Republic.

Agrippa, Menenius, consul 503 B.C., mediator between the *plebs* and the nobles in 493 B.C., in which year he died.

Atilius Regulus. See note on *Serranus*, chap. 10.

CHAPTER 20. *Philus*, a sceptical academician, one of the circle of Scipio Africanus the younger.

Laelius, the intimate friend of the younger Africanus.

Crassus, the famous financier, triumvir with Caesar and Pompey.

CHAPTER 22. *Crates*. See Florida 14 for some account of him. The rest of the poem on his wallet is preserved by Diog. Laert. vi. 5. 1, but is scarcely worth quoting.

Antisthenes, the founder of the Cynic school of philosophy, flourished circa 366 B.C. He was the teacher of Diogenes.

CHAPTER 24. *Lollianus Avitus*. See note on Claudius Maximus, chap. 1.

Anacharsis, a Scythian prince who travelled far in search of knowledge. He came to Athens in the time of Solon and created a great impression by his wisdom.

Meletides (or more properly Melitides) was an Athenian of proverbial stupidity, whose name was synonymous for blockhead. Eustathius on Odyss. x. 552, says that he could not count above five or distinguish between his father and mother!

Syphax, king of the Massaesyli in W. Numidia, fought for the Carthaginians during the second Punic war, and was finally defeated and captured by Scipio in 203 B.C. After his fall *Masinissa*, King of the Massyli, was left supreme in Numidia.

duumvir. The chief magistrates in a *colonia* were styled *duumviri iure dicundo.*

the dignity of my position. This is generally interpreted as meaning that Apuleius himself had become *duumvir.* It is more likely, considering his age and his continued absences from Madaura, that it means merely the position acquired for him by his father's distinguished office.

CHAPTER 25. *Magician is the Persian word for priest.* 'The name *magi* applied to all workers of miracles, strictly designates the priests of Mazdeism, and well-attested tradition made certain Persians the inventors of genuine magic, the magic which the Middle Ages styled the black art. If they did not invent it, for it is as old as humanity, they were at least the first to give magic a doctrinal basis and to assign it a place in a well-defined theological system.... By the Alexandrian period, books attributed to Zoroaster, Hostanes, and Hystaspes were translated into Greek.' Cumont, Les Religions Orientales dans le Paganisme Romain, p. 227. Cp. Pliny, N.H. xxx. 7. *Plato*, Alcibiades i. 121 E.

Zoroaster, son of Oromazes, the founder of the ancient religion of Persia (Mazdeism).

CHAPTER 26. *Plato.* The allusion is to Charmides, p. 157 A. Socrates offers Charmides a charm to cure the headache. But the charm will do more than cure the headache. 'I learnt it, when serving with the army, of one of the physicians of the Thracian King Zamolxis. He was one of those who are said to give immortality. This Thracian said to me ... "Zamolxis, our king, who is also a god, says that as you ought not to attempt to cure the eyes without the head or the head without the eyes, so neither ought you to attempt to cure the body without the soul,"... "For all good and evil, whether in the body or in human nature, originates, as he declared, in the soul, and overflows from thence, as from the head into the eyes. And therefore if the head and body are to be well, you must begin by curing the soul; that is the first thing. And the cure has to be effected by the use of certain charms, *and these charms are fair words*; and by them temperance is implanted in the soul, and where temperance is, there health is speedily implanted, not only to the head, but to the whole body."' (Jowett's Translation.) Apuleius scarcely makes a fair use of Plato's words, which he has so far detached from their context as to give them almost entirely a new meaning.

Zamolxis, probably an indigenous deity of the Getae. Greek legend made him a Getan slave of Pythagoras, who on manumission went home, became priest of the chief deity of the Getae, and taught the Pythagorean doctrine of the immortality of the soul.

CHAPTER 27. *Anaxagoras* of Clazomenae, born about 499 B.C. He came to Athens and had great influence there, being the friend of Pericles and

Euripides. He was, however, banished for unorthodoxy and died at Lampsacus aged 72.

Leucippus, the founder of the atomic theory. His exact date and place of birth are uncertain.

Democritus of Abdera, born about 450 B.C. He developed the atomic theory of Leucippus.

Epicurus, like Democritus and Leucippus, maintained the atomic theory. Cp. note on chap. 15.

Epimenides, a seer and prophet of Crete who purified Athens of the plague with which she was afflicted in consequence of the crime of Cylon, circa 596 B.C.

Ostanes, or Hostanes, a famous semi-fabulous magician of Persia.

the 'purifications' of Empedocles. Empedocles of Agrigentum (flourished circa 450 B.C.) wrote a poem of 3,000 lines, entitled 'purifications' (καθαρμοί). In this he recommended good moral conduct as a means of averting epidemics and other evils. But as a fragment quoted by Diog. Laert. viii. 59, shows, he claimed also to have power over the winds.

the 'demon' of Socrates, the divine sign or voice (δαιμόνιον), which is represented by Socrates as having guided his actions, is never spoken of by him in terms that would lead us to suppose that he regarded it as a familiar spirit, though it is so treated by later writers (e.g. Plutarch, de genio Socratis, and Apuleius, de deo Socratis).

the 'good' of Plato. The reference is probably to the identification of τὸ ἀγαθόν with the δημιουργός the creator spoken of in the Timaeus.

CHAPTER 30. *Vergil.* Cp. Ecl. viii. 64-82. Aen. iv. 513-16.

the wondrous talisman. The allusion is to the *hippomanes* or growth said to be found on the forehead of a new-born foal. Unless the mother was prevented she devoured it.

Theocritus, sc. Id. ii.

Homer, e.g. the adventures with Circe.

Orpheus. See the Orphica (Abel), *Fr.* 172; Argonaut. 955 sqq. Lithica 172 sqq.

Laevius. The MSS. give Laelius. But no poet Laelius is known. There was, however, a poet *Laevius* at the beginning of the first century B.C.

the lover's knot. The Latin is *antipathes*, explained by Abt (Apologie des Apuleius, p. 103) as *quod mutuum affectum provocat*.

the magic wheel spun rapidly to draw the beloved to the lover. Cp. Theocr. ii. 30. 'And as this brazen wheel spins, so may Delphis be spun by Aphrodite to my door.'

nails. Portions of the beloved were valuable ingredients in charms. Cp. Apul. Metamorph. bk. iii, 16, 17, where hair from the beloved's head is required.

ribbons used as fillets during the ritual. Cp. chap. 30, 'soft garlands.'

the two-tailed lizard. Theocr. ii. 57, testifies to the use of the lizard as a love charm. A magic papyrus from Egypt (Griffiths Thompson, col. xiii (23), p. 97) mentions a two-tailed lizard as an ingredient in a charm to cause death.

the charm that glads, &c., sc. *hippomanes*; see note on preceding page.

CHAPTER 31. *Homer*. Iliad xi. 741. Odyssey iv. 229.

Proteus. Odyssey iv. 364.

Ulysses. Odyssey xi. 25.

Aeolus. Odyssey x. 19.

Helen. Odyssey iv. 59.

Circe. Odyssey x. 234.

Venus. Iliad xiv. 214.

Mercury. Cp. the magic hymn contained in a magical papyrus (Papyr. Lond. 46. 414). 'Thou art told of as foreknower of the fates and as the godlike dream sending oracles both by day and night.'

Trivia = Hecate.

Salacia, a Roman sea-goddess, the wife of Neptune.

Portumnus, the Roman harbour-god.

CHAPTER 32. *Menelaus*. Hom. Odyss. iv. 368.

CHAPTER 35. *A shell for the making of a will*. The pun *testa ad testamentum* cannot be reproduced in English.

seaweed for an ague. Here again there is an untranslatable jest. *Alga* (seaweed) suggests *algere*, 'to be cold,' one of the symptoms of the ague (*querceram*).

CHAPTER 36. *Theophrastus* of Eresus, the favourite pupil of Aristotle.

Eudemus of Rhodes, also a disciple of Aristotle.

Lycon of Troas, a distinguished Peripatetic philosopher (floruit circa 272 B.C.).

CHAPTER 39. *Quintus Ennius*, 239-169 B.C. The lines which follow are all that survive of the Hedyphagetica. They seem to be closely imitated from the Gastronomia of Archestratus quoted by Athenaeus iii, pp. 92. 300. 318. There is great uncertainty as to the text, and but few of the fish mentioned can be identified with any certainty.

CHAPTER 40. *Homer.* Odyssey xix. 456.

CHAPTER 41. *And yet it is a greater crime*, &c. An allusion to the vegetarianism of the Pythagoreans and others.

Nicander of Colophon, an Alexandrian didactic poet. The θηριακά survives, is over 1,000 lines long, and deals with the bites of wild beasts.

Plato. The words are not actually found in Plato's extant works; Apuleius is probably slightly misquoting Timaeus 59*c*.

CHAPTER 42. *Varro* (Marcus Terentius), 116-28 B.C. The most learned and voluminous of Roman authors.

an image of Mercury. Clearly the reference is to some such practice as that of 'screeing' in the ink-pool. Cp. Kinglake, Eothen, chap. 18.

Cato (the famous Marcus Cato, see chap. 17, note) was priest of Apollo and received offerings to the god.

CHAPTER 43. *Plato.* Sympos. 202, where δαίμονες are spoken of as powers 'which interpret and convey to the gods the prayers and sacrifices of men and to men the commands and rewards of gods.' Also cp. de deo Socratis, chap. 6.

fair and unblemished of body. Beauty and virginity are insisted on in various passages in the magical papyri (see Abt op. cit., p. 185) as necessary in the boy through whom the god is to speak. Cp. also Benvenuto Cellini's Autobiography (Symond's Translation, p. 126, ed. 1901).

Pythagoras. 'I think also it was said by the Pythagoreans respecting those who teach for the sake of reward, that they show themselves to be worse than statuaries or those artists who perform their work sitting. For these, when some one orders them to make a statue of Hermes, search for wood adapted to the reception of the proper form; but those pretend that they can readily produce the works of virtue from every nature.' Iamblichus, Life of Pythagoras, chap. 34 (Taylor's Translation).

CHAPTER 44. *as might fairly be produced at a sacrifice*, &c. The divination is preceded by sacrifice just as in Benvenuto Cellini (loc. cit.) the sorcerer first burns incense. The head is touched as being the source from which the oracle is to proceed (*arx et regia*, chap. 50). The clean robe is necessary, to ritual purity and is mentioned more than once in the magic papyri.

CHAPTER 45. *Gagates* is, according to Pliny, N.H. xxxvi. 141, 2, a black smooth stone, resembling pumice. It is light and fragile and differs but little from wood. When powdered it emits a strong odour; when burned it smells sulphurous, and, wonderful to relate, it is kindled by water and extinguished by oil.

CHAPTER 47. *Twelve Tables*. In this, the earliest Roman code, punishment was imposed on any person *qui fruges excantassit*, or *qui malum carmen incantassit*. Pliny, N.H. xxviii. 2. 17.

Quindecimvirs. The *quindecimviri sacris faciundis* were priests of Apollo and had charge of the Sibylline books.

CHAPTER 49. *The Timaeus*, pp. 82-6.

The *three powers that make up the soul* are those mentioned in the Timaeus, 35 sqq., i.e. *Same*, *Other*, and *Essence*.

CHAPTER 50. *The Comitial sickness*, so called because, if a case of epilepsy occurred during the meeting of the *comitia*, the assembly was immediately broken up.

CHAPTER 51. *The Problems*. Aristot. Fr. ed. Rose, p. 181.

Theophrastus, cp. fragm. 175*w*. Diog. Laert. v. 2. 13.

CHAPTER 52. *Thallus contracts his hands*, &c. 'Thallus manus contrahit, tu patronos.' The pun is (*a*) bad and (*b*) untranslatable into reasonably good English. The literal meaning is 'Thallus contracts his hands, you collect advocates'.

CHAPTER 55. *The comrades of Ulysses*, &c. Odyss. x. 28-55.

Aesculapius. Cp. Florida 18.

the mysteries of father Liber. The mysterious object is probably the mystic casket (*cista*) containing the φάλλος, emblem of fertility.

CHAPTER 56. *The followers of Orpheus and Pythagoras* abstained from the slaying of animals for the service of man. Cp. Herodotus ii. 81.

Mezentius. Cp. Verg. Aen. vii. 647 'contemptor divom'.

CHAPTER 57. *Ulysses*. Odyss i. 58.

CHAPTER 62. *High and low through all the town*. The pun on *oppido*, 'exceedingly,' and *oppido*, 'town,' does not admit of reproduction.

CHAPTER 64. *The Phaedrus*, 247. 'For the immortal souls, when they are at the end of their course, go out and stand upon the back of heaven, and the revolution of the spheres carries them round and they behold the world beyond. Now of the heaven which is above the heavens, no earthly poet has sung or ever will sing in a worthy manner. But I must tell, for I am bound to speak truly when speaking of the truth. The colourless and formless and intangible essence is visible to the mind, which is the only lord of the soul. Circling around this in the region above the heavens is the place of true knowledge.' (Jowett's Translation).

The King. The passage quoted is from Plato, Epist. ii, p. 312 (403). It goes on to say 'and he is the cause of all things that are beautiful'. Compare the νοῦς βασιλεύς identified with the cosmic soul in the Philebus 29E-30A.

CHAPTER 65. *The Laws*, pp. 955, 6. It is possible that μονόξυλον may mean 'of one wood only'.

CHAPTER 66. *Marcus Antonius, Cnaeus Carbo*, &c. Of these *causes célèbres* nothing is known worthy of mention here. Apuleius errs in saying that Mucius accused Albucius. As a matter of fact Albucius accused Mucius on the ground of extortion. Cp. Cic. Brut. 26. 102. For the suit between Metellus and Curio cp. Ascon. in Cornel. 63. Cnaeus Norbanus should probably be Caius Norbanus, and Caius Furius, Lucius Fufius. Cp. Cic. de Off. ii. 14. 49, de Or. ii. 21. 89, and Cic. Brut. 62. 222, de Off. ii. 14. 50.

CHAPTER 73. *A discourse in public.* Fragments of such discourses are to be found in the Florida.

CHAPTER 75. *His gold rings.* By the time of Hadrian the wearing of a gold ring (*ius anuli aurei*) was no more than a sign of free birth, and the only privilege conferred was that of obtaining office. See *Anulus*, Dict. Ant.

CHAPTER 78. *When you dance in those characters.* Tragedy proper had been replaced on the Roman stage by the *saltica fabula*, in which the *pantomimus* executed a mimetic dance illustrating a libretto sung by a chorus.

CHAPTER 81. *Palamedes* was famous for having detected the pretended madness of Ulysses, by which he sought to avoid going upon the expedition to Troy. Ulysses was ploughing and Palamedes placed the infant Telemachus in front of the ploughshare. Ulysses revealed his sanity by stopping the plough.

Sisyphus, King of Corinth, was famous as a master of all manner of deceit, outwitting even the arch-thief Autolycus. He was finally cast into Tartarus for having discovered the amour of Zeus with the nymph Aegina.

Eurybates (or Eurybatus) coupled with Phrynondas by Plato (Protagoras 327). He was an Ephesian sent by Croesus to Greece with a large sum of money to hire mercenaries. He betrayed his trust and went over to Cyrus.

Phrynondas, a stranger (probably a Boeotian) who lived at Athens during the Peloponnesian war and became proverbial as a scoundrel.

clowns and pantaloons. *Maccus* and *Bucco* were stock characters in the Atellan farce.

CHAPTER 85. *The viper*. This superstition arises from the fact that the viper does not lay eggs, but is viviparous.

a well-known line. The author is unknown.

CHAPTER 87. *Quite at home in Greek*. See note on chap. 4.

CHAPTER 88. *The line so well known in comedy*. The reading nearest to the MSS. would be παίδων ἐπ' ἀρότῳ, γνησίων ἐπὶ σπορᾷ (Van der Vliet). Unless, however, the phrase παίδων ἐπ' ἀρότῳ γνησίων is a stock phrase which occurred in more than one comedy, which might perhaps be argued from the plural *comoediis*, there can be no doubt that the words ἐπὶ σπορᾷ are interpolated, inasmuch as the line occurs in the fragment of the περικειρομένη of Menander, discovered at Oxyrhynchus by Drs. Greenfell and Hunt (Ox. Pap. ii, No. 211, p. 11 sqq.), and runs as follows

ταύτην γνησίων
παίδων ἐπ' ἀρότῳ σοι δίδωμι. Πολ. λαμβάνω.

Serranus. See note on chap. 10.

CHAPTER 89. *Multiplying by four*. The pun in the word *quadruplator* cannot be reproduced in English. The name was given to a public informer who sued for a fourfold penalty.

a slip in the gesture. Bede (Op. Colon., MDCXII, vol. i, p. 132 *b*) says, 'When you say ten, you will place the nail of the forefinger against the middle joint of the thumb, when you say thirty, you will join the nails of thumb and forefinger in a gentle embrace.' Here the MSS. read *adperisse*, which suggests *aperuisse*. But *aperuisse* does not naturally express the gesture described by Bede, and Helm's emendation *adgessisse* seems necessary.

CHAPTER 90. *Carmendas, Damigeron*, &c. *Carmendas* is unknown. *Damigeron* is mentioned elsewhere as a magician (Tertull. de Anima, 57), but nothing is known of him. *Moses* appears as a magician in the magical papyri (Griffiths Thompson pap. col. v, p. 47 (13)). The miracles wrought by Moses in Egypt sufficiently account for this. *Jannes*, one of the Egyptian magicians worsted by Moses. Cp. Epistle to Timothy ii. 3. 8. *Apollobex*, a magician named *Apollobeches* is mentioned by Pliny, N.H. xxx. 9, as also is *Dardanus*. For *Ostanes* and *Zoroaster* see chaps. 25 and 27, notes.

CHAPTER 95. *Cato*, the earliest of the great orators of Rome: for his excellences see Cicero, Brutus, 65 sqq. (Cp. note on chap. 17).

Laelius, see note on chap. 20. Cicero selects *lenitas* as the chief characteristic of his style (de Orat. iii. 7. 28).

Gracchus (Caius Sempronius) was famous for the fire of his oratory (cp. Cic. Brut. 125, 126, de Orat. iii. 56. 214).

Caesar is generally praised chiefly for *elegantia* in his oratory, rather than for his warmth (cp. Cic. Brut. 252, 261, Quint. x. 1. 114).

Hortensius, Cicero's chief rival: a master of the Asiatic style (cp. Cic. Brut. 228, 9. 302, 3. 325-8).

Calvus, a contemporary of Cicero. One of the chief representatives of the Attic style (cp. Cic. Brut. 283).

Sallust, the famous historian.

CHAPTER 98. *The garb of manhood.* He had already assumed the *toga virilis*, cp. chap. 88. This must be taken metaphorically = 'You let him behave like a man.'

CHAPTER 101. *He who can plead in court*, &c. There is a play on *perorare* (= to plead in court) and *exorare* (= to win over his mother by prayer).

CHAPTER 102. *What a criminal use of love-philtres*, &c. There is a pun on *veneficium* and *beneficium* which cannot be reproduced.

THE FLORIDA

CHAPTER 2. *Plautus*. Truculentus, ii. 6. 8.

the great poet. Homer, Iliad, iii. 12.

CHAPTER 3. *Vergil*. Ecl. iii. 27.

CHAPTER 4. *Antigenidas*, a famous musician of the first half of the fourth century B.C. Others attribute the grievance to his pupil Ismenias. This story is also told by Dio Chrysostom xlix.

CHAPTER 6. *Nabataea*, a district at the north-east end of the Red Sea.

Arsaces, a king of Persia (perhaps Artaxerxes II, 379 B.C.) from whom the Parthian kings traced their descent. Here *Arsacidae* = Parthians.

Ityraea, a district under Mount Hermon to the north of Bashan.

Ganges. The quotation is from Statius, Silvae, ii. 4. 25.

wash gold. Lat. *colare* = to strain, sift.

CHAPTER 7. *Alexander.* This story of his portraits is told by many writers, though Lysippus is substituted for Polycletus by the more accurate, inasmuch as Polycletus was a sculptor of the fifth century, and contemporary with Pheidias! This is quite characteristic of Apuleius.

Apelles, the greatest of Greek painters, floruit circa 332 B.C.

Pyrgoteles, one of the most famous gem-engravers of Greece. Little is known of him beyond this story.

the professor's gown. Cp. Aulus Gellius, ix. 2, where a man with a long beard and huge cloak tries to persuade Herodes Atticus that he is a philosopher. Herodes replies, 'I see the cloak and the gown, but not the philosopher.'

CHAPTER 9. *Hippias of Elis*, one of the early sophists (middle of the fifth century B.C.); cp. Plat. Hipp. Min. 368 B.

the reciter's wand. It was the custom in Greece for a reciter to hold in his hand a wand or ῥάβδος.

Severianus, proconsul of Africa between 161 and 169 A.D., as is shown by the words *the two Caesars*, M. Aurelius and L. Verus.

CHAPTER 10. *The Sun.* The passage quoted is from some unknown tragedy, perhaps a Phoenissae, cp. Eur. Phoen. 1.

Mercury. Those born under Mercury had a 'mercurial' disposition, those under Mars a 'martial' temper (cp. *ignita*).

other divine influences that lie midway. Cp. note on Apologia, chap. 43.

CHAPTER 11. *darnel.* The quotation is from Vergil, Georgic i. 154. Cp. also Ecl. v. 37.

CHAPTER 14. *Crates.* Cp. Florida 22, and Apologia, chap. 22.

CHAPTER 15. *Polycrates*, floruit circa 530 B.C.

Pythagoras. See note on Apologia, chap. 4.

Pherecydes. See note on Apologia, ch. 27.

Anaximander, an Ionian philosopher, born 610 B.C.

Epimenides. See note on Apologia, chap. 27.

Creophylus, an early epic poet, reputed author of the 'Capture of Oechalia', which he was said to have received from Homer as the dowry of the latter's daughter.

Leodamas. Nothing is known of this Leodamas. Apuleius may have made a slip and written Leodamas for Hermodamas, who is mentioned by Diog. Laert. viii. 2, as the descendant of Creophylus.

CHAPTER 16. *Philemon* was a writer of the 'new', not the 'middle' comedy.

'farewell' and 'applaud'. Cp. the well-known epitaph:—'iam mea peracta, mox vestra agetur fabula: valete et plaudite.'

Aemilianus Strabo was *consul suffectus* in 156 A.D. See Prosopographia imp. Rom. part 3. nr. 674, p. 275.

while breath still, &c., from Vergil, Aeneid iv. 336.

priesthood of the province of Africa. See Introduction, p. 12.

CHAPTER 17. *Scipio Orfitus,* proconsul of Africa, 163, 4 A.D. See Prosopographia imp. Rom. part 1, nr. 1184, p. 464.

Orpheus to woods, &c., from Vergil, Eclogue vii. 56.

CHAPTER 18. *the tragic poet.* Unknown.

Plautus. Truculentus, prologue 1-3.

no rose without a thorn. The Latin is *ubi uber, ibi tuber.* Wherever you get rich soil, there you will find pignuts.

the council of Africa was theoretically an association for the worship of the imperial house. It had some political importance, however, inasmuch as it might criticize the governor and forward its criticisms to the Emperor at Rome.

Protagoras, a famous sophist of Abdera (latter half of fifth century).

dilemma. See note on Apologia, chap. 9, *self-inconsistency.* A closely parallel story is told of Corax and Tisias, rhetoricians slightly earlier in date.

Thales of Miletus, the first of the great mathematicians and physical philosophers of Greece: one of the seven sages. He flourished towards the end of the seventh century B.C.

CHAPTER 19. *Asclepiades,* a famous physician from Bithynia, of the first half of the first century B.C.

CHAPTER 20. *The first cup,* &c. The wise author of this saying was, according to Diog. Laert, i. 72, Anacharsis.

Empedocles. See note on Apologia, chap. 27.

Epicharmus, a famous comic poet of Megara in Sicily. He flourished early in the fifth century B.C.

Xenocrates. Diog. Laert. mentions five writers of this name, none of them of any great importance. It is possible that we should read *Xenophanes*, who, according to Diog. Laert. ix. 10, wrote *silli*, a form of lampoon or satire. He was the founder of the Eleatic school and probably flourished about 500 B.C.

CHAPTER 22. *Crates pure and simple*, i.e. by his renunciation of the world described in chap. 15.

CHAPTER 24. The MSS. give this as a prologue to the de deo Socratis. It belongs, however, manifestly to the Florida.

Aristippus, founder of the Cyrenaic school, a friend and younger contemporary of Socrates.

FOOTNOTES

[1] See Introd. to my translation of *Metamorphoses*.

[2] See *Apol.* 68 sqq.

[3] He regarded Plato as his master above all others. We find *Platonicus* attached to him as an honorific title in the MSS.

[4] For a vivacious exposition of this view cf. Monceaux, *Les Africains*. Paris, 1894.

[5] See the chapter on Apuleius in Norden's admirable work, *Die antike Kunstprosa*, Leipzig, 1898.

[6] I conjecture: *de morte cognati adolescentis subito tacens tanti criminis descriptione destitit, ne tamen omnino desistere calumnia magiam, &c.*

[7] Shelley's translation.

[8] *facti* MSS.

[9] *et simplicia*, vulgo.

[10] MSS. *Laelius*.

[11] *Saurae inlices bicodulae*. Helm, wrongly I think, places a comma between *saurae* and *inlices*.

[12] *merguntur* MSS.

[13] *ne pergam* (Helm).

[14] *vocem* (Colvius).

[15] *seu* (Casaubon).

[16] *putredo* (conj. Helm).

[17] *a bria* (Hildebrand).

[18] *rictum diductum* (Jahn).

[19] *ructus popinam* (Pricaeus).

[20] *depectoribus* (Kronenberg).

[21] *inde* (Acidalius).

[22] *gratum factum* (Van der Vliet).

[23] *iterum* (Riese).

[24] i.e. vowels.

[25] *se ecfert—calumnia se mergit* (Salmasius).

[26] τὴν εἱμαρμένην ἔχω (Rossbach).

[27] *oblivio* (Casaubon).

[28] *is Moses* (Jan. Parrhasius).

[29] *quas vel tu vel quisquis* (Van der Vliet). There is no doubt as to the sense required: the precise correction must remain doubtful.

[30] *quam in omnibus minor Minervae* (H.E.B.).

[31] *post quae* (Beyte).

[32] Omitting Helm's insertion of *praemium* after *quam*.

[33] *semitam* (codd. inferiores).

[34] Omit *qui* inserted by Helm after *ut*.

[35] *frondibus*, cod. Florent. 29. 2 man. primi correctoris.

[36] *inhibens* (Heinsius) *pinnarum eminus* (MSS.).

[37] *fulminis vicem de caelo improvisa, simul.* Van der Vliet places a comma after *vicem* and gives none after *improvisa*.

[38] *libentius ego* (MSS.).

[39] *denique ceteri commemorant* (MSS.).

[40] *clausulae* vulgo.

[41] *Daedalum* (Krüger).

[42] *corvinam quidem si audias idem conantem, crocire non loqui.* The text is corrupt, Van der Vliet's suggestion probably gives the correct sense.

[43] *qui* vulgo.

[44] *Anacreonteum* vulgo.

[45] *ceterum multum abest* (MSS.).

[46] Omitting *illa* before *Indiae gens est*.

[47] *statos ambitus* (Krüger).

[48] *mortalibus* MSS. *late pecuniis* (Stewech).

[49] *loqui* (Van der Vliet).

[50] The reading is uncertain. Van der Vliet's suggestion seems to give the outline of the sense desired.

[51] *unam gratiam* vulgo.

[52] *vobis comprobari* (Krüger).

[53] *non minus uereor quam intellego* (Krüger).

[54] *nunc postea vota omnia mea* (MSS.).

[55] om. *honos* following MSS.

[56] *quantum spero* (MSS.).

[57] om. *et negotiosis* following MSS.

[58] *quid si etiam* (Krüger).

[59] *cassus labor supervacaneo studio. Plurifariam superatur*, (MSS.). The reading is uncertain, but the above punctuation will yield adequate sense.

[60] om. *usquam libentius* with MSS.

[61] *Thalem ... suasisse* (MSS.).

[62] *uti* (Beyte) *cognosceret more ingenii* (MSS.). *more ingenii* may be corrupt. If it may stand, it must mean 'as his nature prompted him', i.e. to satisfy his curiosity.

[63] *litteratoris, ruditate* (Krüger).

[64] *modificabor, tanto a vobis in maius tolletur.* So all editions before Van der Vliet. The words *tanto ... tolletur* have no MS. support, but some such insertion is necessary for the sense.

www.ingramcontent.com/pod-product-compliance
Ingram Content Group UK Ltd.
Pitfield, Milton Keynes, MK11 3LW, UK
UKHW031835270325
456796UK00003B/412